NOSTALGIC DAYS

Further Reminiscences of a Great Western Fireman

by
Harold Gasson

Oxford Publishing Co · Oxford

ISBN 0 86093 079 3

ACKNOWLEDGEMENTS

It is not possible to write a book about Great Western steam locomotives without a great deal of help from a number of very kind people. In this regard I have been very fortunate, for without that help, this book would not have been possible.

Special thanks are due to the following:—

Mrs. Clare Sellen, for her beautiful poetry;

Ken Robinson, my photographic adviser;

Vic Smith, ex-Old Oak Common fireman;

Bert Edmonds, retired Old Oak Common driver, and Vic's footplate mate,

Bill Bishop, retired Eastleigh break-down steam crane driver;

Roy Oxendale of the Quainton Road Society;

Colin Judge who has always had faith in my writings,

and all the very kind readers who wrote and asked "when is the next book due?", for without them, it would not be worthwhile.

Typesetting by Getset (BTS) Ltd, Eynsham, Oxford

Printed in the City of Oxford
by B. H. Blackwell Ltd

Published by
Oxford Publishing Co.
8 The Roundway, Headington
Oxford

Cover photographs: Front by A. T. Mathews
Back by Peter Zabek

Foreword

When I sat down and compiled my first book *Firing Days* it was to fulfil an ambition of many years standing. The three years of hard work had been worthwhile when the letters began to arrive from readers who had enjoyed it, and with those letters came requests for a further reading.

From these requests the second book *Footplate Days* was born, and as I packed my typewriter away, I thought that perhaps readers would have had enough of my reminiscences of Great Western footplate work, but the very welcome letters kept arriving, not only from all parts of the United Kingdom but also from as far away as America and New Zealand, and these letters always asked the same question: when will book three be ready?

Book three grew in the same way as *Footplate Days* with little pieces of information coming together, and conversations with other ex-footplate men that began "Do you remember?".

"Did I remember?" How could I ever forget? Writing this book brought it all back, particularly those conversations with my dear old Uncle, Bert Edmonds, one of the long retired "Top Link" drivers from Old Oak Common Shed.

The final problem came with choosing a title. It would be nice to keep the "Days" series, and as I was reading my introduction to *Footplate Days* I found it: 'Nostalgia' — an apt description of what this book is all about.

Again my dear wife Betty took kindly to my disappearing act into my den, and but for her valuable proof reading, unbiased criticism, and the endless cups of coffee, I would have given up, because I found that a typewriter can be much more demanding than a "Castle".

Harold Gasson
1980

Chapter One

What could it have been like those few short years ago when the Great Western steam locomotive was as much a part of the landscape as the elm tree, when, for example, on 25th March 1948 an engine history sheet was filled in at Swindon for a 4-6-0 named *Wightwick Hall* priced at £9,648 (including the tender)? That particular story ended on 17th July 1964 after this locomotive ran only 640,645 miles, and the history sheet finished with the words 'sold to Woodham's Bros. Barry'. There was a time when the strange world of the footplate could be viewed at any main line station. The thick powerful lines of a 'King' or the sleek beauty of the 'Castles' was sure to draw a crowd of small boys, admiring males, and if the fireman looked a bit of a lad, the ladies too! Even the fussing brash little pannier tank snorting up and down in the goods yard could draw such attention. The only locomotive left out of this admiration was the humble freight locomotive, the 'cart horse' and the men that worked them.

What was this unnoticed world of freight movement where no speed records were made and no performances produced worth writing about in the railway press? It was nothing but punching away up adverse gradients day in, day out, or pitching and swaying down banks with the handbrake screwed down. Here locomotive working was far removed from the glamour of the expresses, and yet those men running the expresses would have been at home on the big lumbering 'twenty-eights' and 'forty-threes'. They had come this way themselves; for there was still excitement and satisfaction in making a good run with a heavy freight train, and it began at home, in dressing into overalls, pulling on boots, that last warm embrace, then going to work.

One August afternoon I plodded down the dusty cinder path towards Didcot locomotive shed with a distinct feeling of injustice. It was hot, very hot, on this afternoon, my jacket was over my shoulder, hooked through the loop with my finger, my 'Grimsby' box swinging from my right hand. Already I could feel the beads of perspiration forming under the leather band of my cap.

1

There was no joy in my heart as I walked into the cathedral coolness of the shed to meet my driver, Ted Hurle. We had begun the week on the early turn, looking forward to the week-end with anticipation. I should have now been strolling along the river bank between Reading and Tilehurst with my lovely young lady, and Ted would have been quietly cycling over the Berkshire Downs towards a certain village, where, when the pub was open he could pour pints down very thirsty stable lads in exchange for "fortune-making information". But the best laid plans go astray, progressive overtime during the week, and the re-turning to each duty after twelve hours rest had brought us both to this late start.

I 'booked on' and found Ted waiting for me in the enginemen's rest room. I was bemoaning our bad luck, thinking of my young lady stuck in the hostel with all those lecherous young off-duty firemen in residence, but Ted with the experience of the older man, had the answer to my gloom. As he explained, doing all that overtime had increased the savings account, consequently the wedding was that much nearer, and he would be that much more better off by not pouring pints down the bottomless throats of stable lads who gave tips about fast 'gee-gees' that were not so fast when he placed his hard earned money on them.

Perhaps this 4.30p.m. relief turn was not so bad after all. We had no locomotive to prepare, perhaps we would relieve a goods heading for Swindon, then a quiet pint in the Staff Association Club before heading for home and an early finish. I began to brighten up, after all there was always Sunday not even used up yet.

We walked back up the path together, over the crossing, past the yawning well of the subway steps, and down the Up Yard to the Control Office. Bob Beck the controller, was standing in the doorway, his jacket off, his tie loosened, mopping his brow with his handkerchief. The little wooden building that served as Control Office and enginemen's rest room was like an oven.

The Up Yard pilot engine No. 5735 stood simmering nearby, its cab empty, for both driver and fireman were sitting on an old sleeper in the shade of a coal wagon on the next road. Further down the yard the ring of couplings could be heard as the Centre Pilot eased up a long string of wagons for the shunter to join up.

Bob informed me that the 10.30a.m. Banbury to Westbury had left Oxford and he required us to relieve the Banbury men. Not so bad, a gentle 'doddle' on the Up relief to Reading, and with a bit of luck an early finish after all. Ted and I made our way back up the yard, over the shed exit road, over the Down Loop and both Oxford main lines to the Up 'Gully'. We sat on the grass bank waiting for our train to arrive, and before long a column of dirty smoke and steam could be seen behind the trees towards North Junction. We both looked back. Could I hear the harsh roar of a blower above the distant exhaust from that chimney?

The 10.30a.m. Banbury came slowly into view, at its head a tired travel-worn old 'forty-three' workhorse, rocking from side to side, steam leaking from her cylinder pressure valves, a volcano of black smoke erupting from her chimney as she clawed her way painfully round the curve towards us, her long train curving away behind her, the wheels squealing in protest as the flanges bit into the bullhead rail.

No. 4377 came to a rest with her tender opposite the water column. She looked huge, the high level of ballast had placed her footplate twelve feet above us. She was dirty with years of neglect, her spokes caked with grime, her framing was so thick with dirt that her wheels had worn a rim in a half circle of hardened sludge, and she smelt of old age. Ted swung the water column round as the Banbury fireman scrambled over the coal to lift up the tender flap. As I moved forward to climb up onto her footplate, the injector gave a cough and a grunt, spitting out half a gallon of scalding hot water onto the sleepers, splashing one of my boots. I stepped back smartly, right into a two inch deep puddle of slurry, and it shot up inside my trouser leg and ran down into my boot.

A welcome indeed. Ted gave a rich chuckle. It was a situation he could appreciate, and he began to open the water feed valve on the column. He was so entertained by my misfortune he forgot that the Up 'Gully' water column was a local 'old sore'. The square on the valve handle was worn to a half circle, and as he wound round that valve it came off the spindle and clouted him on the knee-cap. The old saying "he who laughs last" was true after all! I side-stepped the spitting injector overflow pipe and climbed up, tapping the feed valve on the tender as I passed. The injector picked up cleanly, leaving just a dribble to trickle onto the ballast. The ritual of relieving was over quickly. Ted exchanged and received the necessary information on the state of the train and the engine, whilst the fireman assured me that she was steaming freely, and although she rode a bit rough she was a 'good un'. However it was with almost indecent haste that they climbed down and walked off.

3

The tank began to overflow, so I climbed down, shut off the water, then went back up the tender steps and threw off the bag, while Ted went round oiling the slide-bars and glands. I shovelled forward some coal, enough to see us to Reading, so that when Ted returned to the cab we were ready to go. Ted yanked on the whistle chain to blow up a 'crow' and the chain snapped in his hand. I should not have laughed, because he used my cap to lift the whistle rod. The points slid over, and the signal dropped with a thump to route us on to the Up relief line.

The ejector was opened blowing off the brakes, then Ted applied the vacuum to allow me to ease the tender hand brake, he then blew off the brakes again and lifted the regulator as I fully unwound the hand brake. We began to move as the couplings tightened up one at a time until the whole of the train was on the move. As she took up the weight Ted gave her full regulator, opening and closing, waiting for the slightest sign of a slip. It was then this poor old lady began to talk to us. As each cylinder took a charge of steam she lurched over and began to groan, as her valves came back she gave a piercing squeal, her big reversing lever began to jump in the ratchet, and the red needle on her faded steam pressure gauge quivered with every blow as her great side rod came slowly up and over.

Ted increased her oil by giving the sight feed lubricator half a turn as we pulled painfully out of the 'Gully' and on to the Up relief. The signalmen at Didcot East Junction quickly ran to slide shut their windows before we filled that long greenhouse with smoke and ash. As the guard's van cleared the points Ted was able to pull back the reverser a few notches and ease down her regulator. No. 4377 began to cease her violent protesting and by the time we were passing Moreton Yard the regulator was tapped down a bit more and she began to settle down to her own pace.

I began firing her now, repairing the holes torn from her firebox, nursing her back to health as we ambled along letting the old lady take her time. At this pace she was almost comfortable to ride on although she knocked in her axle boxes, her cab rattled and shook, her reverser threatened to jump out of the ratchet, and she had begun to lose steam pressure. I had not been mistaken, I had heard a blower back at Didcot. It was time to give her some help, so with half a turn of blower to keep her burning well, I piled some coal into her. After another half turn on the fireman's friend "the blower", she had come round to the blowing off mark within a mile, so the live steam injector was put on to top up her boiler. She should have accepted this without any trouble. After all, I had been told that she was a 'good-un' but a glance up at that faded steam pressure gauge told me that she did not like cold water spraying into her boiler one little bit. Whew! I had lost forty pounds of pressure between Moreton and Aston Tirrold.

It was time to take some drastic action. I lifted the pricker out of the tender rack and Ted stood back on the running plate as I swung it round. It slid into the firebox and I began to stir her up, ramming that pricker right down to the front end, pulling it back through the fire, the barb ripping great furrows of red hot coal, the smaller pieces dancing up and down with the blast. The heat came back into the cab in a searing wave. I withdrew the red hot pricker and returned it to the rack, then lifted the front damper just off its face. Now we would see what she was made of.

I began to fire her, packing the back corners of the firebox, building up on that thick bed of fire. Ted pulled her back another notch on the reverser and the blast softened, she was taking less steam in her valves and pistons. I said a silent prayer to Allah, and, bless her, she began to respond. The steam pressure needle began to climb and the cab settled down now to a quiet grinding. We had found that happy spot applicable to all steam locomotives, the spot where she would run and steam to the best advantage.

As we ran up towards Cholsey I turned on the exhaust injector and hot water began to spray into her boiler. We were winning, she liked this treatment. Ted and I grinned at each other, after all it was only to Reading, or so Bob Beck had said and another poor blighter would have to pound her up to the top of Savernake. We swept under the bridge, sitting on our tip-up seats, swaying with the movement of the cab into an ocean of golden corn fields which stretched for miles either side of us.

Our old "forty-three" was settling down, holding her own now. She had ceased her groaning and squealing as the extra lubrication reached her valves and pistons. I began to fire her with regularity, flap down, a swing of the shovel, then flap up. Each shovelful produced a puff of black smoke from her chimney to roll back over the cab and be swept over the fields, leaving behind the distinctive pungent aroma of the burning of good Welsh Marine coal.

The exhaust injector was singing away keeping the water level dancing up and down just below the top nut in the gauge glass. I was neither gaining nor losing on that water level, everything was just right now. We swept through South Stoke with a cheery wave to the lady coming out of the back door of the Pub below, with a pile of washing in her arms. We then ran through the chalk cutting towards Goring, round the slight curve, clattering through the station picking up speed nicely now for the run over the water troughs. They came into view, four narrow ribbons of water shimmering in the sunshine, curving gently round between the rails towards Purley. I eased down the water scoop, just skimming the water topping up the tank. We then headed towards Pangbourne, round the tree covered chalk cliffs that curved into Pangbourne station, past the red tiled Mock Tudor houses peeping between the trees, then out into the flat meadow land that ran alongside the river.

Cabin cruisers cut through the placid water, raising a bow wave which spread across the river and started the moored boats bobbing in a frenzy of curtsey movements. The skippers with grim determination gripped the steering wheels, their white caps tilted Navy style as they navigated their craft on through the complex of shipping, with their ladies in scanty bikinis laid out on the cabin roofs. They neither glanced up nor altered course. We were an intrusion, a reminder of a working world far, far away, to be forgotten.

I began to clear up ready to stop at Reading, but as Scours Lane signals came into view we saw that we were to continue running on the Up relief, not as we had expected into the Goods Loop. A horrible doubt began to form, and became a reality. We had been "conned", we were going through. The poor blighters pounding up to Savernake would not be Reading men, it would be us!

Between Scours Lane and Reading West Junction the lookout boy gave us a friendly wave. The lookout boy was a familiar sight to enginemen. From his lofty position in the top of a tree he could see up the lane to the Oxford road, and all over the scrubland. He was the sentinel, the early warning system, protecting the fifty or so males squatting around a blanket at an illicit game of Pitch and Toss. It was worth our blast on the whistle and frantic gestures towards the road were answered with the classic two fingered sign; "cry Wolf" had been played out, but it was worth it just to see one or two round the blanket jump up all ready to run. Did the local "coppers" ever catch that game, I wonder?

Ted shut the regulator and put his left foot up on the bar at the front of the reverser, knocked up the clip with the palm of his hand and eased that big lever forward. We drifted over the running lines and as soon as we felt the rise of the bank he gave her a little steam, increasing as the weight began to pull. We mounted this curving rise towards Reading West. Below us in the triangle, Reading locomotive shed lay under a pall of drifting smoke from the chimneys of the rows of 'Castles', 'Halls', 'twenty-eights', and the sisters of our old girl. Two small boys watched us with interest in the lane below, their spotter's books all ready. They turned away, as we did not have a great curving nameplate on our top frame, we were of no importance to them.

We rambled over the Oxford Road bridge, through the sleepered platform of Reading West station baking in the sun and under the overhang of trees. Trees, deep green and heavy with leaf. Chestnut trees with broad leaves and sycamore shimmering in the slight breeze, welcome shadow indeed. In a few more months they would shed those leaves to fall over the rails, giving the 'Kings' and 'Castles' some moments of anguish before the sand was spread to give the speeding wheels welcomed grip. Soon we were passing Southcote Junction and heading West towards the sun.

As we ran alongside the Bath road busy with traffic, I began to fire her again. This time with serious deliberation as this was not the gentle amble up the relief line to Reading. This road to the West I knew well, enough to know that apart from the odd mile or so of "flat" railway at Aldermaston and Newbury, it was a solid grind for the next 32 miles, culminating in the heavy pull from Bedwyn to the summit at Savernake.

Ted dropped the lever forward one notch and gave her half regulator, then he stood back on the running plate to catch the slight breeze. I began to sweat as I shovelled in the coal, the drips from my forehead staining the floorboards in single drops. I removed my overall jacket and hung up my cap. My shirt was already wet through and sticking to my back and by the time we reached Savernake those floorboards would have a six inch wet band between the firebox and tender.

Through Theale I hung over the side to cool off, and watched the Tiger Moths on their "circuit and bump" training programme. In the hot air they came floating over the hedges, the engines cut back, then with a sharp burst on the throttle they would bounce over the grass landing strip. I returned to the shovel. The exhaust injector had been on from Reading West so it was time to "top up" over Aldermaston troughs. I lowered the scoop further down this time and the blade bit deep into the water, spraying the excess out through the tender wheels. I felt like shouting "come on, come on, fill up, fill up", as the float crept slowly up the gauge. We were running out of trough and needed every drop of water. At last we were full and with a bit of luck we could keep going through Newbury instead of stopping for water.

Round the slight curve we came, through the empty sleeper platforms of Newbury Racecourse station, the scene of the loss of so much of Ted's money. We passed the lattice steelwork of the foot bridges and all distant signals were off through Newbury middle road. The safety valve began to lift as we came pounding through the station. We blew a 'crow' on the whistle to our mates on the return Winchester passenger standing in the Bay, then our exhaust hit the road bridge at Newbury West with a "Whoof". Our side rods were knocking with a thump as that great knuckle end came up and over. The wagons and box vans rattling along behind caused a swirling cloud of straw, old labels and other bits of railway debris and dust to rise and obliterate the quiet calm of a country station.

We were approaching Enborne Junction now, with the twin rails of our beloved Winchester Branch curving away to the left. What price now for the peace and quiet of the rolling Hampshire Downs on this lovely summer evening. Our old 'forty-three' gave a kick and a lurch as she passed over the junction points, as if to remind us we were heading West not South. As we passed under the signal box window the faint tinkle of the block bell came over the noise of our engine.

'Ding ding', 'Train on line' to Kintbury. On up the bank gently rising, the bark from the chimney growing deeper as the train started to drag. We passed through the lush green meadows of the Kennet Valley, full of sleek cows munching contentedly away, tails swishing lazily from side to side as they gazed at us so passively. I was firing now without a break, the coal going into that raging furnace was digested almost at once, and slowly the boiler level began to creep up.

A quick sharp rise up through Hungerford followed and as we passed over the tops of the houses, we could look down into the back gardens and onto the rows of runner beans and potatoes, or perhaps the quiet haven of a pub lawn with the pint pots standing on the rustic tables, and envy the lucky lads drinking. One even held up his glass in a salute, rubbing it in. He was probably an off-duty footplate man. We returned that gesture with a rude code on the whistle, and we were right, he understood.

We began to feel the climb in earnest now, but the old lady was holding up well enough. My boiler water level was well up so I could afford to concentrate on maintaining a full head of steam for the ferocious last few miles beyond Grafton. As we passed through Bedwyn I fired her for the last time, and the firebox was full, so once over the top of Savernake she would roll all the way down to Westbury with just a few shovelfuls to keep on the boil.

Once through Bedwyn, Ted had to drop the lever down again and give her full regulator. I shut off the exhaust injector, but even then she began to drop in steam pressure. Perhaps it was because I had put the shovel down and the sweat stains on the floorboards were beginning to dry.

As Grafton came into view she was flat out with the lever right down, regulator full open, and as her speed dropped off she began rocking, first over on one side, then over to the other side. Each cylinder was taking as much steam as it would hold, back and fore, right down to the springs, the exhaust exploding with a roar out of her chimney. It was a wicked way to treat this poor old lady, to thrash her for mile after grinding mile, but it was the only way, had she slipped, we would have stalled, so she had to be thrashed as she had never been before. Looking back over the events years later, I can still feel for that old 'forty-three'.

No. 4377 had been built at Swindon in 1911 with superheaters, vacuum brakes, two 18½ inch cylinders and a Churchward boiler to supply them, and was termed as a mixed traffic engine. Here she was doing the work of a 'twenty-eight' and it must have been an awful sight as we clawed our way through Grafton, yard by yard. As I levelled the fire over with the pricker, it was a white hot incandescent mass dancing in time with the blast. Again as I withdrew the pricker Ted stood clear. It was white from the tip to half way up its length where it dulled to a cherry red and tiny specks of coal dust ignited as they touched. In that searing heat they instantly burned out to cascade in a shower of stars which were extinguished before they reached the worn, stained floorboards.

The cab was shaking to bits and there was a half inch gap between it and the boiler, the safety valve bonnet was rattling, the frame was jumping, and above it all that great reversing lever was jumping so badly that Ted rammed the coal pick in the quadrant. I closed the firebox doors and at once they began to slam up against the firebox, the air shrieking as it passed through. The exhaust was one gigantic column of power climbing forty feet into the blue summer sky to be caught by the breeze and sent rolling and tumbling down into the valley behind us. The cinders rolled and swirled along the van roofs, rattling on the curved roofs down into the gutterings then falling down to join the burnt out cinders of other years and other struggles between man and machine.

All at once it was over, we were through Savernake station and as her nose dipped down, so did the water in the boiler. I put on the live steam injector and the water began to bob back in sight. We had won, the despair of the last few miles was behind us. We had made it because we were a close team working together, and without that we would have failed. It was recovery time now and I hung over the side of the cab to feel the cool breeze on my brow wash over me to channel down the front of my shirt which by now was moulded to my back like a second skin, I was whacked. I watched Burbage sidings slide by, as Ted closed the regulator then lifted it a shade giving her just enough steam to lubricate her valves and pistons. I heard the firebox doors being opened and Ted gestured me to sit down as he placed the tea can on the shovel, for there is nothing like a scalding hot cup of tea after a good sweat. I looked ahead to see Pewsey come up towards us, and as the sinking sun caught us, that old locomotive became a thing of beauty, she was poetry in motion as the pistons slid back and forth, the rod glistening between the slide bars, I slurped that cup of tea and had started on the second before Ted could wet his lips with the first. There was a hint of the word 'guts' from somewhere over his side and the reply of 'nuts' from my corner as we sailed over the little hump just short of Woodborough. We then drifted down to Patney, the wagons coasting along behind.

As we swept round the slight curve I looked back beyond the vans and wagons, rattling and swaying as they danced along to see the first flickering light in the bullseye as our guard lit his side lights.

With the sun sinking, the shadows of the engine and train ran with us in a soft outline, sliding over the meadows and corn fields, slipping over hedges and ditches in complete harmony, almost a mirror reflection of the original, the feather of steam from the safety valve, a wisp of steam escaped from the whistle; the injector waste pipe dribbled water; my movement between engine and tender as I reached for the teacan; all these were reproduced in silhouette. It was a peaceful time, the shadows began to lengthen and our old engine began to change shape. She became fatter, her chimney taller, and in my imagination she began to take on the shape of a Broad Gauge Gooch locomotive of one hundred years earlier.

All enginemen had favourite spots to enjoy on any route, particularly during the summer months and we were now coming up to one of them, the long swoop down the bank to Lavington. Mile after mile of twisting and curving rail with nothing to do but sit on the tip-up seat and enjoy the run. The old 'forty-three' was also enjoying it. She ran free without knocking, groaning or protesting, with just the swish of her wheels going round, and the heavy "click-click" as she passed over the rail joints accompanied by the slapping of her vacuum pump.

There were other places to be enjoyed for me anyway. There was the swoop down from Tackley bank heading towards Banbury where the line twisted and curved as we hammered through Heyford station with the severe camber tilting us over and the cylinder skimming the platform edge. Another favourite was the Up road at Wolvercote running alongside the canal. One could see the polished brass on the gaily painted narrow-boats chugging their way softly through the still water. If you were lucky you might see the lightning flash of the kingfisher, crimson and blue as he plunged in and out of the water near the lock, a minnow wriggling in his long beak, so swift there was hardly a ripple in the water.

There was the dull deep rumbling when passing over Nuneham bridge, looking down on the willows which shaded the river, bending gracefully to touch the water. One might see a moorhen with her chicks, paddling away from the bank, her bow wave spreading out over the placid flow of the river, her chicks bobbing up and down in her wake. Sometimes we would see the dragonflies skipping, swooping and skidding over the surface, to vanish, as a flash of silver snatches them from sight, leaving only a widening pool of ripples.

It is only now with nostalgia for the days of the steam locomotive and the deep-seated urge to write about those happy days that I can begin to appreciate what the Great Western was all about. I was part of a family. I had, in common with so many steam firemen before me, followed father's footsteps onto the footplate. I was a G.W. man and, looking back over the years, I can still feel the pride I had and still hold in that knowledge. I had been in no way instrumental in placing the 'Great' into the Western, but had in my small way helped to keep it there. The men who had made the Western 'Great' were gone, but I can remember the Didcot members. They were the men who had fired on the Broad Gauge, the young firemen of the 1880 period. Men like Joe Beckenham and George Bowering, Arthur Hitchcock and Jack Wiley, Jackie Wilkins and Harry Cudmore, men who had fired to the Broad Gauge drivers, and those drivers had in turn fired to the first Great Western drivers. They were the lads who could remember the Gooch locomotives. They had taken them out of the old wooden shed at Didcot, to be followed by the 'Armstrongs'. The old gentlemen I remembered had followed with the 'Deans' and 'Churchwards'. They had fired to drivers who wore a bowler hat and sported heavy black beards. Their uniform was a black serge jacket, thick corduroy trousers, and the inevitable dangling watch chain, threaded through the waistcoat buttons to anchor down in the pocket. A watch, and what a watch it was. I still have one; the casing made out of gunmetal of such proportions as to defy all the elements including the pull out regulator and reversing lever of the 'Iron Dukes'.

It was the day of gleaming brass, burnished copper, tallowed paintwork and open cabs. Joe and his mates not only cleaned those gigantic eight foot driving wheels but also the spokes, and, behind the spokes. The inside cylinder covers were scoured with brick dust until they shone equal to a chrome finish. Smokebox rings, brackets, dart handles, handrails and buffers all received the same treatment. Then they climbed up on to the smokebox foot step, on to the grab rail, until they could stand on top of the boiler barrel and clasp that tall chimney with the embrace of an ardent lover as they polished the copper band. Even the whistles protruding from the weather board sparkled in the sunshine.

No wonder those big handsome broad gauge locomotives stand square and proud in the old photographs, and the enginemen too stand square and proud. These big strong silent men fitted the locomotives like a glove. There was only one thing in these photographs missing and that was not even a smile, not even a trace of a twinkle in the eyes, not a hint of humour. But the reason was there. They were not only in the process of making the Western Great, but they were doing it with no uniform issue, for a working shift of 12 hours, for three shillings and sixpence. Yet they were at that time the elite in the ranks of the working man. Harry Cudmore told me that William Dean had a sense of humour alright. As these lads were so busy building up the Great Western he thought that they might like a change in the working conditions, so he cut the "tanner" off the three bob and gave them another two hours to work, and that is why, I think, photographs show them without a smile! The sheds somehow got together, not an easy task with the long hours and shift duties, and decided to send a deputation to see Mr. Dean at Swindon. It is recorded, 'A meek and humble memorial was presented to the GWR Directors late in 1879 asking them to receive a deputation from the men' and from this they obtained a meeting. The minutes read as follows, 'It is still more sad to reflect that the deputation came, some of them nervously, as if they were going to trial by Assize, and they left empty'. All that they had asked for was a 10 hour day and that it be recognised that 150 miles for the passenger men and 120 miles for the goods men, constitute a day's work.

They carried on, there was not much else they could do. Driver Thomas Shuter was fined 7/6d for running an axle box hot. Such was their pride in the job that driver Jack Almond ran the Bristol express from Paddington to Didcot, 53 miles from start to stop in 47 minutes. But there were complaints, one driver spoke of being on Pilot duties for 40 hours, another for periods of 20 and 24 hours and as such his faculties were impaired and his energy abated. A locomotive inspector was appointed to look into these complaints and his findings were made known. He had found cases of drivers being on duty for 36 hours but reported that 'when in a siding they had the opportunity of going to sleep on their engines'. There is no record of what would have been the outcome if he had caught them asleep on their engines, but sleep they must have had and their energy replaced, because as Joe used to say to my old dad, they somehow found the time and energy to make sure that there were plenty of young recruits to replace them when retirement came round.

They were craftsmen, proud of their calling. If William Dean was not amused of their idea of a day's work, they were proud of the locomotives he gave them to work on, proud enough to carry on the tradition of enginemanship which enabled the design and development of the Swindon built locomotive to reach perfection. Joe and his mates were in a unique situation although they did not know it at the time, because their working life on the footplate spread from the last of the Gooch engines right through to the 'Castles' and 'Kings'. It was as if Orville Wright flew the Kitty Hawk and carried on to pilot a Jumbo Jet.

This transition from broad gauge to standard gauge and on to the big locomotive was mercifully a gentle one. The classes of

13

locomotive to pass through their hands made it the golden years of Swindon power, and there can never again be a period of time quite like it. In handling this vast build up and changeover of locomotive power, they put the 'Great' into the Great Western for all time and this wealth of locomotive working was handed over to my father's generation.

As this generation served their long hard apprenticeship of firing, the knowledge soaked in a little bit at a time. This knowledge coupled with the arrival of the 'Saints', 'Stars', 'Castles' and 'Kings' began to pay dividends and Great Western locomotive power was on the march. That vast reservoir of knowledge was then passed on to my generation, and we seized on it with eagerness and used it, but for such a short time. With the arrival of the diesels, at least for me, brought the end of the line.

It must have been a wonderful time in those early days of 1880 apart from the pay and working conditions. Joe saw many miles of track laid as the system expanded, whilst I, at the other end of the scale, saw so many miles lifted. Those men were in on the building of the Didcot to Newbury branch, opened on 12th April 1882 and the extension through to Winchester on 1st May 1885. They began working the branch with the little Armstrong 0-6-0 tanks, the open cabbed 2-4-0 Metropolitan tanks and the 3230 class 2-4-0 tender engines.

I awoke with a start! After that day dreaming of the past, we had slipped through Lavington and Ted began to give her a little steam as the signal lamps of Edington and Bratton loomed up. I gave her a little coal, enough to see us into the yard and on the shed. We clattered over the points of Heywood Road Junction, the curving Westbury cut-off racing away into the darkness and then we crept through the station and into the yard. The shunter slid his shunting pole between the tender and first wagon, there was a loud metallic ringing sound as the coupling swung down and we were parted from our train. Five minutes later we were leaving our dear old 'forty-three' on the ash road.

I looked back at her as we walked away and felt compassion for her. She was old, dirty and rough, she had known better days, to some she was just a lump of scrap, but we had hammered the living daylights out of her and she had not let us down. A little bit of me remained on her, perhaps I would never see her again but I would always remember her. Now, years later as I write and think about her, I can see her, a tired old lady desperately in need of the rest she so richly deserved.

14

We had a bite to eat in the enginemen's cabin then reported to the foreman. His eyes lit up as did all foremen's eyes when an unexpected crew turned up. It was the sort of look members of the inquisition must have given their victims; a "what can I sort out for this lot" look. But I am being unkind, he did sort us out a job, to relieve some Weymouth men and take a light engine back to Swindon via Trowbridge.

We took off running light with a Hall, No. 4960 *Pyle Hall* scheduled for Swindon Works and a complete rebuild. We left her on Swindon shed just after midnight and as we had now been seven and a half hours messing about with engines, it was time to have a good meal and go home. There was nothing due on the 'Up' until the 1.40 a.m. Swindon parcels, so we set off for the canteen where I sat on my own, tucking into with gusto, a plate of bacon, eggs and fried bread swimming in half an inch of thick grease, topped off with a rich dark brown cup of three hour old tea. Poor old Ted couldn't face it. He sat at the other end of the canteen crunching a curled up scrap of dry toast and burping each time he looked my way. I mopped up the grease with a slice of bread. Ted turned away, perhaps the digestive systems of older people deteriorate over the years, or, so I suggested to him. His reply was most uncomplimentary.

We caught the Parcels as far as Foxhall Junction where the Swindon driver slowed down to allow us to scramble off, then we walked over to the shed and booked off at 2.30 a.m.

Walking up Haydon road towards home I began to reflect on our pay and conditions compared with the old fellows of 1880. Working from the new Didcot shed over the Newbury branch I used to think sometimes that I was hard done by, belting a 'twenty-eight' with a full load or that old 'forty-three' we had left back at Westbury. After all it had been a fair day's work or perhaps by contemporary standards I was justified in thinking so. The standard of 1880 and their 3/6d a day for 120 miles was a lot of mileage for a small engine. To Westbury via Reading or from Didcot to Southampton and back, with a full load each way and a firebox three times the size of the old locomotives was a fair comparison. As for wages and hours, well, we just had completed an average week as follows.

Monday   We ran from Didcot to Swindon with No. 2803, returning through Reading with No. 2876, then back to Didcot with No. 3121 a little 0-6-0 LMS

15

	engine, having covered 86 miles on a duty of 12½ hours.
Tuesday	We went to Southampton and returned with No. 6864 *Dymock Grange*, covering the 116 miles in 14 hours.
Wednesday	Our duty was to Old Oak Common with No. 2926 *Saint Nicholas* returning with No. 4703, covering the 103 miles in 11½ hours.
Thursday	We travelled North to Banbury with No. 3837, back to Swindon with No. 4909 *Blakesley Hall* then back up to Didcot on No. 8404, one of the class 8Fs built at Swindon for the LMS. A distance of 124 miles and a 12 hour duty.
Friday	This of course was with that old 'forty-three' to Westbury and by the time we arrived home another 116 miles and 10 hours had passed. Therefore eleven locomotives had passed through our hands, covering about 545 miles over a period of duty of 60 hours during that week.

My pay for that week came to £4.1s.2d or roughly a bob an hour. Looking at that old pay slip I see that I did have some stoppages, nine shillings and 6d. in all made up of: 4/11d National Health Insurance, 2/6d Life Assurance, 1d Staff Association, 1d Railway Convalescent Homes, and 1/11d Mutual Aid Society. Income Tax? I must have paid some although there is no record on the slip, but I can't see any government allowing a young single man to have all that money to throw about, can you!

The next week I worked on the Stationary boiler. A duty of 48 hours with no overtime and no night rate. My pay after the stoppages came to £2.9s.8d. It was the week my cigarettes gave way to the 'roll-up', and yet now *I* would gladly pay *them* to be able to swing a shovel again.

Chapter Two

Is it a good thing to look back? I think perhaps it is; a little nostalgia gives pleasure to those of us who can remember, and provides information to younger folk. Looking back is a habit of each generation and I am no exception. When I was a boy the senior drivers would talk for hours to a willing listener; Joe Beckenham would talk of working on the Dean 7ft. 8in. 4-2-2s with affection, of running from Paddington to Didcot in 49 minutes with No. 3065 *Duke of Connaught* and from Paddington to Oxford with No. 3252 *Duke of Cornwall* in 62 minutes. I've done it the other way with a 'Castle' and we have gone like hell in the night to reach Paddington in the hour from Oxford.

It was part of the main line that Joe loved. He would talk of shutting off through Acton and just letting her run, with no outside connecting rod to flash round, no loose coupling pins and slack bearings to clank and knock, no bucketing and swaying on the footplate, just that great single driving wheel spinning round with the effortless grace of a gyroscope. My uncle Bert Edmonds started firing on the 'Dukes' at Oxford, where they had such a job in climbing up the bank from the shed to the station. The shed pilot would be standing by to give them a shove. At 6.05 p.m. every evening the shed and station staff would be out, waiting for the 'up' Worcester and 'down' Paddington to pass, the big 'Singles' gliding along and passing halfway through the station like a zephyr of wind.

Joe would speak with revulsion when referring to the convertibles and one in particular, a 4-4-0 tender engine No. 3527. She was for some time his regular engine beginning life as a broad gauge tank, rebuilt from an 0-4-2 into an 0-4-4 standard tank, then with typical Swindon skill of rebuilding she ended up as No. 3527. To look at she was not unlike a 'Bulldog', working out her life on the Didcot to Winchester branch, but although she steamed freely enough she rode badly so Joe hated her. She was a convertible and that was enough. He would compare her with the 'Singles', knocking the former and enthusing over the latter, but I can see now a lot of his chat was "tongue in cheek" for he knew only too well that a lot of the 'Singles' left Swindon as 2-2-2 broad gauge engines.

I was far too young at the time to take in all that Joe could tell me. The very fact that I was on the footplate with him was enough to keep me completely absorbed in all around me, but when I look at photographs of the 'Singles', I can appreciate the love Joe had for them. That great polished dome, the brass band on the splasher arching over the big wheel in a strip of gold, and in the centre of that imposing wheel the axle box burnished up to glitter in the sunshine, they were indeed a handsome sight. I can just remember what a polished dome looked like, it must have been when I was very young. I know I had been taken down to the old wooden shed at Didcot where my old dad had met Joe, his regular driver and they had taken me onto the footplate of their engine No. 3454 *Skylark*. On the next road stood No. 3272 *Amyas* with a brightly polished dome. Joe held me up and I remember our reflections were as distorted as if looking into a trick fairground mirror. There are incidents which stand out in a small boy's memory with such sharpness that it lasts over a lifetime. I can remember this one with such clarity that it could have been a few days ago. The image of a fat, comically distorted boy held in the arms of an equally grotesque little man, and in the background, *Skylark's* cab and tender curving away on either side, reflected in that sparkling brass dome.

Another incident was to see these fine old gentlemen on their way down Station Hill towards the shed. They did not go to work as other men, they 'proceeded' to go "On Duty" — they were Great Western enginemen, they were the master craftsmen of a steam age on their way to practise their skill on the footplate of the Great Western's beautiful green engines. It was of no consequence if it was in the early hours, or the engine waiting their attention was an old 'Armstrong'. The pattern was the same, they were on a par with the village policeman, respectable, sober God-fearing men. They strode down the hill, boots polished, overalls starched, jacket brushed, cap peak shining and set square, the crossed watch chain threaded through a waistcoat button hole, the small medallion and watch key hanging from a small piece of chain, swinging gently with the ponderous gait of their walk.

Even noticing a small boy was something, but a greeting was acknowledged by a grave nod of the head, and yet I was to find them to be the most kindly of men. One, driver Jack Wiley, petrified me. He was such a large man, and I was such a small boy. When I did overcome my fear of him it was to relieve him of sixpence, and to find there was nothing about him that suggested that he ate small boys for dinner. I had gone down to the old wooden shed with father, for it was Thursday, and pay day, and when he was home on that day it was an accepted part of life to go with him, as indeed did the sons of other enginemen. It was, in a way, the first step the Great Western made to ensure the continuity of future enginemen for I cannot remember any restrictions placed in the way of the sons of the footplate men.

We arrived at the shed just as Jack stopped with a little saddle tank engine, who had dropped on shed to collect his pay. I looked up at this giant of a man and squeezed closer to father.

The method of payment was peculiar to Great Western sheds, and lasted into my working days. We would first go to the timekeeper's counter, not unlike a station booking office, where father would collect his pay check. This was an oval brass disc, that had 'Great Western Loco' stamped round the face, with the number of the disc in the middle, in father's case number 50. I can remember that although these brass checks were only used once a week they were all polished up. I was to find in later years that a cleaner's duties did not stop at boilers, wheels and big dollops of cotton waste. Father handed his check over to the pay clerk, and in return he received a small round tin box, also with the number 50 stamped on it. Inside this box was his pay, the notes folded over, leaving a little room in the middle for the odd silver and copper coins. It was a long way off from the pay packet. Those tins had been in use for years, in the days when a pound note kept its value. Father would extract the notes and silver, with the odd coppers becoming my pocket money.

With their usual efficiency the Great Western provided a large wooden box for the collection of the empty tin boxes. This was about the size of a tea chest, made from heavy timber. Its back was hinged to allow the removal of the tins, but the top was not open or flat, it was angled down in a sharp 'V' with a slot in the middle, just wide enough to allow the empty tins to pass through. Enginemen would drop their tins down so that they would roll down and into the box. Small boys now had to earn the coppers they had just received, it was a ritual practised by every father. I was given the empty tin, placed back a few yards, and expected to toss that tin into the box. It was not so easy, with the angled top causing the tins to bounce out again. On this particular Thursday I could not get father's tin into the box, and tears of despair clouded my eyes and I wanted to go and hide. Then along came Jack Wiley. He bent down, gave me his empty tin, and held up a sixpence, without a word being spoken. Despair turned to desperation as I threw that tin high into the air and it dropped cleanly through the slot and into the box with a clatter. Jack was delighted, and he handed over the sixpence. Holding my hand he walked with me over to his engine, informing father that he could collect me at the station. We stopped at the bottom step, Jack preceding me up onto the footplate. He paused on each step until he reached the top, then he eased his prominent front portion over the handrails and followed it in. By this time I had climbed up two steps, while Jack had turned round and a rich 'Brummie' accent so unfamiliar to my ears came out of the sky to say, "Youall coom up 'ere with me, my dook". Then two enormous great hands came down under my arms to pluck me off the steps, up and over the handrails, and deposit me on the fireman's seat. I can remember my legs dangling from that seat, my finger nails digging tightly into the wood underneath me, and seeing a large hole containing a fiery furnace. Then there was a movement of levers and we began to move. The furnace began to suck in air, almost pulling me from my perch into that hole. Jack must have seen my concern, because he lifted a chain and a flap came up shutting off that fire. On arriving at the station, his hands came under my arms, and again I sailed up and over, to be placed onto the platform and the safety of father's warm hand.

That sixpence had been earned, and it was some years before I was to earn another from the Loco staff. Again I had gone to the shed on a Thursday, but by this time the new shed. I suppose as an eight year old I was beginning to feel my feet, strong enough to take up the challenge from Fred Holt that I could not turn his engine, or earn sixpence for doing so — well, we would see.

The locomotive was No. 3807 *County Kilkenny* standing on

Number 2 road. I climbed up onto her high footplate and rode down to the turntable with Fred, where he balanced her to perfection. She was so 'spot-on' that as we walked back towards the end of the turntable our weight caused it to tilt. Fred gave me a start as I began to push, then stood back, and I felt the weight of the locomotive. Then I was away, pushing with a great deal of effort. It was a surprise, a good strong gust of wind would have turned her. I looked back at Fred with a grin on my face, that sixpence was as good as in my pocket. Fred stood there with one hand on his hip, the other holding his cap while he scratched his head. He was what is known as non-plussed, but there was an explanation. Neither of us knew the cause at the time, and as Fred now began to follow me round he could not see what was going on at the other end. What had happened, of course, was that someone was on at the other end, pushing, and with the bulk of *County Kilkenny* on the turntable, plus the bridging girders, they were always out of sight. There had been some artful collusion between my old dad and Arthur Hitchcock, as much to help me as to confuse Fred. Whilst Fred and I had been busy backing the locomotive off Number 2 road, they had gone through the shed and out at the bottom end, to wait behind the Lifting Shop. As Fred and I climbed off the footplate they had run down our blind side to the other end of the turntable, ready to push.

It was years before Fred found out. I was firing to him one day, and he brought up the subject of how I turned that engine on my own. I told him how it had been done and he gave me a grin and said I had not seen the last of *County Kilkenny*. It was the only 'County' that I can remember as they had all been scrapped long before I joined the Great Western, and they had gone with the grateful thanks of the enginemen. As rough riders they had earned a reputation, although my old chap had said that they would steam and pull well enough. Yet as this class of locomotive was being broken up at Swindon, the Southern were building an identical engine in the 'School's' class which was to prove to be one of the finest 4-4-0s in the world. It was a beautiful locomotive and a credit to Mr. Maunsell and his design team. With all the interchange trials to come, I now regret that there was no interchange of enginemen, as I would have loved to have had a go on a 'School's'.

Fred was as good as his word, I had not seen the last of *County Kilkenny*. He took me home with him when we had finished our duty, and there in his front room over the mantelshelf arched that great nameplate from *County Kilkenny*. It held pride of place, the focal point of the whole room. The sun shone through the window and bathed it in a soft golden glow, the richness of the deep green paintwork and the thin red outlining accentuating the heavy brass letters. Dead she might be, but part of her lived on to find a good home. That nameplate was Fred's pride and joy and he lavished as much care on it as he did his garden, and his garden was a showpiece.

Fred is gone too now, and the nameplate with him. But 32 years later, from a source far removed from railways, I was given a Great Western engineman's pocket book, and imagine my delight on opening it to find on the inside cover the words 'Fred Holt — Didcot Loco'. So over the years he had reached out and touched me, and it was fitting that the book had found a good home, if only I could trace that nameplate to go with it!

In my boyhood days, Didcot had just about every kind of Great Western engine to be seen. The 'Dean Goods', 'Atbaras', 'Flowers', 'Badmintons', 'Dukes', 'Counties' and 'Bulldogs', some of which survived for me to work on and now I look back with affection. I can recall No. 3269 *Dartmoor*, No. 3267 *Cornishman*, No. 3290 *Severn*, No. 3291 *Thames*, and a whole swarm of 'Dean Goods' soon to be replaced by the wonderful little Collett 22XX class. Indeed No. 2259 and No. 2254 had already arrived, and what joy they gave to a fireman after years of working the old locomotives. An engine fresh from Swindon shops after a complete overhaul was a treat indeed, but to have a brand new design was something special. My old dad said that it was a pleasure to go to work knowing that one of the new 'twenty-two's' was booked for the duty. It could be argued that I was to some extent, biased towards Great Western locomotives, but in those happy days of fine steam locos., as a Great Western fireman I placed myself in the same class as the owner of a Rolls. There was an alternative of sorts, of course, and I was fortunate to be firing when the Great Western had a few 'foreign' engines on the stock book.

There were the Stanier 8Fs, with big gold LMS letters painted on the tender, the eighty-fours, we called them. As all the 84XX class had the small plate on the front frame stamped 'Built Swindon', we treated them as Great Western engines fitted with left hand drive. There were USA Transportation Corps 2-8-0s of Major J.W.Marsh — hulking great locomotives with the footplate comfort of a Pullman coach. The Southern 'Moguls' from Mr. Urie's stable, and the beautiful locomotive from Mr. Billinton's 'Remembrance' class. All very fine engines, but, as good as they were, it was a warm comfortable feeling to climb back on to the familiar Great Western footplate.

Mr. Churchward could be likened to a race horse breeder, for when he introduced the first of what later became the 'Saint' class, No. 100 *William Dean* in 1902, he began the first of a long line of thoroughbreds. With the expertise of Swindon in re-designing and re-building, the resulting crossbreeds produced another line of thoroughbreds, each class of locomotive becoming a success in its own right. The 'Hall' class which in turn produced the 'Grange' and the 'Manor' classes was a perfect example. Mr. Churchward was, in my opinion, the one man since George Stephenson to achieve such a far reaching impact on the design of the 'big' main line locomotive. It was indeed fortunate that he was succeeded by Mr. C.B. Collett, who carried on the Churchward tradition to such good effect.

It has been reported that when a Footplate Inspector was asked to name his favourite locomotive, he said that given a stud of Churchward 47XX and Collett 'Granges', he could cover all the requirements of the Traffic Department. This statement brought some dismay to the gathering, who expected him to enthuse on the merits of the 'Castles' and the 'Kings', but he was right. The big 47XX class and the 'Grange' could have dealt with almost all that came their way. But with respect, from a fireman's point of view, I would add just one more engine to his choice, the Collett 22XX class. These could cover the branch line workings that would have ruled out the 47XXs, and at the same time, were available to shunt out goods yards that would have caused the 'Grange' a little embarrassment, still being able to cope with light main line duties. This fine little locomotive was introduced in 1930 as a 'light mixed traffic' engine intended to replace the veteran 'Dean Goods'. This was not the case. The 'Dean Goods' although almost fifty years young were indestructible, and some would outlast the steam era. What the 22XX class did was to complement the 'Dean Goods', then consolidate and establish itself as a distinctive class in its own right.

The 22XX was a compact little locomotive. In this day and age it would be called a 'Mini' but the 22XX was not a mass produced means of transport, it was a baby 'Castle' with the front bogie missing. The A.T.C. ramp was naked to the eye, as if to give the impression that it was there to stop the high smokebox, perched up on the saddle, from tipping forward. This was an optical illusion, for fitted with the 'Castle' cab, and the small 3000 gallon tender, it was an attractive little engine, and loved by the drivers and firemen. A few were paired with the 4000 gallon ex-W.D. tender, and this marriage turned a little beauty into an ugly duckling. One of our engines at Didcot No. 2252 was fitted with an ex-W.D. tender, and although she steamed as freely as her sisters, she ran like a coal tub. In fact, when she was running tender first, one could, with good reason, think it was a weed killer train approaching.

For a small engine the cab was a delight, large and spacious, identical to the large 2-6-0's, except that instead of the combination of four quadrant dampers, they had the simple up and down front and rear dampers secured by slotting them onto a cross peg, and the vacuum ejector was fitted with the standard steam-brake attachment. There was no exhaust injector, in its place there was a small cone live steam injector on the left hand side, which was ample to cope with the demands on the boiler.

As with all small Great Western engines, 45 minutes was allowed for preparation, although in common with most firemen I liked an hour, so I would arrive on duty early to give me this extra time. Providing there was enough fire left in the box to spread over the firebars, the fire could be built up gently, using the back damper wide open and the blower on just enough to draw air into the firebox. The boiler would generate steam so quickly one could stand and watch the pressure gauge and see the needle move up the scale, but there was no time to hang about, the sand and smokebox had to be checked, making sure the former was full and working, and the latter was empty and tight. It was best to check that the front damper was closed before leaving the footplate, as when the driver was up behind the big ends oiling the motion he would have his back pressed up tight against the front of the firebox. I would think that those sand boxes were as simple as one could get in locomotive design. Providing the sand was dry the gravity feed would place the sand just where it was wanted, even in a gale. Not that the 22XX was in the habit of picking up its feet, but when it did it was like a small volcano erupting up the chimney.

We used our allocation of 22XXs mostly on the Didcot-Newbury-Winchester and Southampton Branch on duties that were tailor made for them, covering both passenger and goods working. To see the 4.30 a.m. Didcot to Winchester goods pulling away from the yard with two Collett 22XXs at the head, was a sight and sound to send the recording enthusiasts of today into rapture. The 'bark' of 'twenty-two's' in full song was a sound never to be forgotten.

We would chuff gently out of the yard with just a hint of the crisp bark associated with this class of engine. On the footplate one could feel her straining to get away as we crossed over the 'Up' and 'Down' relief lines, through the crossover, and then over the 'Up' and 'Down' Main lines, with the wagons snaking and wagging behind us. Then we were onto the Branch, with the six mile climb of 1 in 106 to Churn in front of us, and the fun would begin.

The 28XX class, the 'Halls' and 'Granges', the Stanier 8Fs and the big 'Yanks' would pound up this bank with the action of a beam engine, the big side rods going round with a slow lazy movement, but the little Colletts would attack with the aggressiveness of a terrier dog. They would be placed in full fore gear and full regulator for about half a mile, both chimneys setting up such a racket as to wake up the whole town. Indeed, when duties placed me in bed at this hour, it was possible to trace the progress of the morning Winchester goods, right through to the top of the Berkshire Downs. On reaching the first bridge, both regulators would be eased down, the reverser wound back to the 35% cut off, and both regulators opened to the second valve until the top of the bank was reached.

At this point, the slow feed left hand injector was put on and firing began, and was continued until we reached the top. The back corners of the firebox were packed tight. The shovel dug into the mass of fire to fill any air holes, then under the firebox doors, then built it all up into the Great Western standard 'Haycock'. The blast on the fire would ensure that as fast as the back end was filled it would work its way down. If the flap was used it would be snatched out of the hand as soon as it was halfway up to be slammed up against the ring. The exhaust steam and smoke would curl round the cab roof to pause, between each blast, then to go pouring over the top of the flap into the firebox. When the fire box doors were used they would slam up against the ring, the air sucked through the small hole in a high pitched whistle keeping time with the bark from the chimney. We knew the principles of the ram jet long before Frank Whittle applied it to aircraft.

Once through Upton and into the forty feet deep chalk cuttings, the blast would hit the walls and echo back, adding to the shattered silence of this quiet peaceful place. The night was over, and with the passing of the morning goods the day's work had begun. On a summer morning the rabbits would run ahead, leaping, twisting and scrambling frantically up the sheer cliffs in a blind panic to escape from the bombardment. In the winter, we would plough through heavy snow drifts, the sand lever working overtime to prevent the slip that would end our progress.

The barking chimneys would cause the inch thick telephone wires to dance in tune, shedding their icy casing in long fragments, to be chewed up, pulverised and cast out from under the wheels to fill the cutting with a fog of atomised ice. And yet, the little 'Collett' could cope with it all, for on the passenger workings they became a different locomotive, they would fly along dancing and bouncing, as frisky as a young colt freed from the restriction of a heavy load. The 'Dean Goods' on a three or four coach train would roll up the banks, the little push-over regulator set half way across the guide, the reversing lever set almost in mid-gear, the blast on the fire so soft one could place the shovel right in the firebox to spread the coal round. The Collett 22XX however, would scamper up, the chimney barking away with the rapidity of a machine gun, a wisp of steam from the safety valve whipping back over the coaches. Now and again there would be a sharp twitch under the cab where the rear drivers found a bad patch in the road, to remind us that we had a baby 'Castle' weighing 80 tons as against the 126 tons of big sister. They needed three or four coaches tied on behind them − the 105 to 140 tons was just enough to hold them down and give them something to bite on because without those coaches they would have flown.

We never ran a Collett 'Twenty-two' at speed when light engine running was required. It was far easier to set the regulator just off the jockey valve, and wind the reverser back to 18% cut off, then they would scamper along, giving a little kick on the rear drivers at each facing and trailing points, just to remind us that it was safe to sit down, until the next set of points. In fact, it was only when running light, one was able to use the tip-up seat.

The little Collett was described as a light mixed traffic engine but mixed traffic is far too embracing. They were excellent branch goods engines, superb branch passenger engines and very handy when it came to shunting. I was lucky to come to know these little locomotives as a boy, along with many others such as No. 3448 *Kingfisher* and the two little M.S.W.J. 2-4-0 engines Nos. 1334 and 1335 which were still in service at Didcot when I became an official fireman.

Even when the 'new' shed at Didcot was opened in 1932, there was quite a big staff for a small shed, but nothing compared to Old Oak Common of course. With a locomotive stock of 40, the shed needed 53 drivers and 53 firemen. The shed staff was similar in numbers, and included office staff and foremen, boilersmiths, fitters, mates, shed labourers, firedroppers, in fact all the highly skilled people required to run a locomotive shed. When one took account also of what we then called the Traffic side, Didcot was truly a railway community.

The alternative to railway work of course, was farming, where the delightful delicate aroma of the cowshed, combined with plodding through deep muck to collect cows for milking, or following a team of horses ploughing out the earth for next year's corn. It was no surprise, therefore, to find that most of the local lads came from miles around to exchange the cow shed for a good lungful of burning steam coal. The Frewin brothers came from Wallingford for each duty, and Bill Prior would walk from Chilton village, every bit of six miles, work his duty, and walk home. Such was the calling of the steam locomotive. They were a collection of men that the railway system will never see again. It was much more than just another job, it was a way of life. The 'forty-year man' was commonplace, and the Western was in the golden years of becoming 'Great'.

The pride of the locomotive department was fostered with loving care by the Company itself. As I have written, one began as a very small boy going to the shed on a pay day, and the odd rides at the shed down to the turntable and back. The next step was to arrange that these lads had a chance to handle a shovel. The time to catch them was at about 13 years of age, and although there were never any explicit instructions to locomotive foremen to allow lads onto the engines, there must have been a gentleman's agreement for foremen to look the other way when this occurred.

On most Saturday afternoons I would be with father on the footplate, shunting in the yards with a little pannier tank engine. One Saturday I came into contact with No. 3272 *Amyas* again. Father was covering the Passenger Pilot duties, tailing trains to add or remove box vans, horse boxes, extra coaches, and shunting coaches from the sidings into the bay platforms. An afternoon spent on the footplate of the Passenger Pilot was one of the 'plum perks' enjoyed by drivers' sons. It was a chance to exchange the 'tankie' for a tender engine, and stage three of the Great Western's visions of the future began to ferment.

For the recipient it was an opportunity not to be missed and the training in the art of swinging a shovel began in earnest. On a tender engine there was room, with no scratching and poking about to drop the coal just inside the firebox as with a small tank engine. This was the chance to swing and twist, sliding the shovel over the firebox ring. One became involved and interested, and the succession and acceptance into the close family relationship with the Great Western Locomotive Department was one step nearer. In a couple of years another generation was on their way to Swindon for the examination. There were no advertisements in the papers for railwaymen, as there was no need. Continuity was assured as it was a successful system, proved beyond doubt over the years, and used by each railway company.

The time and location was arranged. In my case it was through Cow Lane bridge, up the path used by the East Junction signalmen, and when the running lines were clear, a signal from father would have me scrambling over the signal wires and rodding, and up onto the footplate. There was never an angry shout from the signal box, as they all knew me to be 'young Harold' going to spend the afternoon with his Dad, and anyway, they had their own sons in the box with them as the Traffic side also knew the value of continuity.

I walked down the road with a feeling of excitement, wearing my old footplate clothes. Father had learnt that mothers do not appreciate their sons coming home from these Saturday jaunts, their school clothes covered in coal and oil stains. I was going on the Passenger Pilot engine with the sure knowledge that it would be a 'big' engine for a change. With luck it could be a 'Hall' or at least a 'forty-three', but as I neared the station an old 'Duke' was pulling out of Number 1 bay platform. She went right up on to the Newbury branch with a string of coaches, then once clear of the points, she propelled them over the main and relief lines into the sidings. I hoped that she was not the Passenger Pilot, but she was. It was poor old *Amyas* waiting for me to join her.

I remember it was a hot afternoon, and with it another incident to store away in the memory, for I discovered that mother made two brands of lemonade, one for the boy, and one for the old chap. She used to boil up a gallon of water, add lemonade crystals and let it stand until it was cool. It was then diluted to taste. My measure was half an inch in the bottom of a tumbler topped up with cold water, but the stuff she provided for father was a man's drink. As I climbed up onto *Amyas* he reached behind the tool

The view from the footplate from the fireman's side of Great Western 'King' class locomotive No. 6000 *King George V* during an Open Day at Hereford.

Author's collection

It might look hard work but I enjoy every minute of it, as seen here pausing 'from duty' of lighting up *King George V* at Hereford.

Author's collection

Always the burning question, 'Shall we take water now, or wait for the next available troughs?' Remember, you would never live down the fact if you ran out!

Author's collection

This is one export I would have liked the government to have banned. 'Castle' class No. 4079, *Pendennis Castle* standing proud and beautifully restored.

Author's collection

ppearing small in comparison to
e might of Great Western 'Hall'
ass No. 6998 *Burton Agnes Hall*,
still feel proud to stand next to
ese monsters that have demanded
much from me.

Author's collection

fine view of Oxford in the days
semaphore signals. The dear old
gine No. 3454 *Skylark* is seen
re on a S.L.S. special awaiting
leave the Up platform.

W. A. Camwell

Two for the price of one! The perfect branch locomotive and one of my favourites, the 'baby Castles', or as we knew them, the 22XX class.

Author's collection

One of the Old Oak Common Top Link crews, Driver Albert Potter with his fireman Jack Peedell seen here on Great Western 'Castle' class No. 5067 *St. Fagans Castle* waiting for the guard's all clear.

Author's collection

Passing Didcot's North Junction is GWR 'Dean Goods' No. 2579 with a local train for Oxford. This one was still going strong right to the end of steam.

OPC collection

A fine view of the footplate of a 'Dean Goods'. Many hours were spent in these cramped conditions, with hardly any protection from the elements, and just enough room to empty that bottle of cold tea!

OPC collection

What did we burn, coal or bricks? Whatever it was, it needed shifting.

OPC collection

Poised for the off, the fireman waits for the 'OK'.

OPC collection

There must be something in there to oil!

OPC collection

No. 3214 in fine condition here at Whitchurch. My old mate Ted Hurle talks with somebody on the platform while his fireman seems to be getting tied up with the water column. Notice the fire devil under the water tower.

OPC collection

One of my photographs that is a personal treasure is depicted here of No. 3376 *River Plym*, one of Didcot's many 'Bulldogs'. Both the driver and fireman were Gassons. A team to be reckoned with!

Author's collection

A BR Class 4, No. 76016 comes to grief on the Newbury to Winchester branch.
Inspector F. Capon

The Whitchurch points claim British Rail Class 4, No. 76017 on 23rd September 1954.

Inspector F. Capon

Bill Bishop lifts No. 76017 out of her hole at Whitchurch with the Eastleigh steam crane on 10th October 1954.

Inspector F. Capon

She's out at last! Bill Bishop (second from left) is still full of cheer after driving his steam crane all night.

Inspector F. Capon

Here a Churchward Mogul No. 5381 is seen with the 12.45 p.m. Didcot to Southampton stopper. This was a through working to Southampton and back for the Didcot enginemen.

Author's collection

Hermitage, one of the many stations on the lovely Didcot and Newbury branch line.

Author's collection

Where it all starts, on shed, with GWR No. 9084 *Isle of Jersey* simmering half in and out.

OPC collection

No steam, no fire and off shed in one hour, it could be a rush.

No. 3393 *Australia* with all hands posing for the cameraman before the hard work ahead.

Watching and dodging the leak. Firemen are always kept busy.

OPC collection

This time the driver gives us a hand with watering 'Manor' class No. 7803 *Barcote Manor* before the long haul ahead.

OPC collection

Waiting for the 'right away'.

OPC collection

The first sit down for two hours as GWR No. 7827 *Lydham Manor* waits for the 'off'.

OPC collection

G.W.R.
ENGINE HISTORY.

No. 6989

Wightwick Hall

Xv ot. 95 2⁴
215

BUILT __25 MAR 1948__   AT ___SWINDON___

Type __4 - 6 - 0.__   LOT __366.__

Diagram A.14.

Weight	T.	C.
Empty	70.	k.
W.O.	75.	16

Including Tender

Cost £ 7,8589
placed per M° 326/5

Including Tender
Boiler £ 4,898
A.T.C.£

Tractive Effort ___27,275 lbs.___

Tank Capacity 4,000 gallons

Cylinders 2. 18½" x 30" (Outside)

REPAIRS

Tender Attached H.O.48	Date Stopped			Station	To Factory			Date set to work			No. of days stopped	Classification of Repair and Miles		Boiler Change or Rep 9241
					Station	Pool	Shops							
4-1-60 Nosca 2909	15	2	50	Worcester Shops.				15	3	50	28.	U.		
"	10	5	50	Hereford.				24	5	50	14.	U.		
HFD. 2533	20	10	50	Swindon Pool.	Fac.		25·10	23	11	60	34	H/G	101.065	C. 9236
9.1.52. 2689	18	3	53	Swindon Pool	Fac		25·3	1	6	53	44	HI.	200.504	C. 9283.
30d3. 2831	8	11	54	Hereford	Sdon	15·11	14·11	13	12	54	35	HG	284.092.	C9.204
13·12·54 4071	26	9	56	Sdon Pool	Fac		28·9	5	11	56	40	H I	373.022	
5/11/56. 2931	11	6	57	Hereford	Sdon	24·6	14·7	5	9	57	83	HC		
9.9.57, 2613	Ext.				Sdon	15·12	17·12	22	1	59	38	HG	468.663	C. 9269
28·12·57 2777														
12·1·59 2772														
Sdon. 5·5·61 4081	5	11	60	Worcester				10	12	60	35	U.		
	6	3	61	"	Sdon	14·3	21·3	5	5	61	60	HG	549 750	C.9.20
	2	8	61	O O C Shops.				23	8	61	21	U		
	27	9	61	Worcester				13	10	61	16	U		
Sdon 17·1·63. 3933	20	10	62	Gloucester	Sdon	12·11	16·11	17	1	63	89	HC	—	—
												90895	

Sold to Woodham Bros.   Barry 17/7/64

as at 28/12/63

CONDEMNED __*1/6/64__   * Late Above, taken from Stock 18/E   13/6/64

TOTAL MILES ___640,645___

Age __16__ years.   Authority __1403ᴬ__   Residual Value £ _____

The Engine History of one that was saved, No. 6989 *Wightwick Hall*.

Author's collection

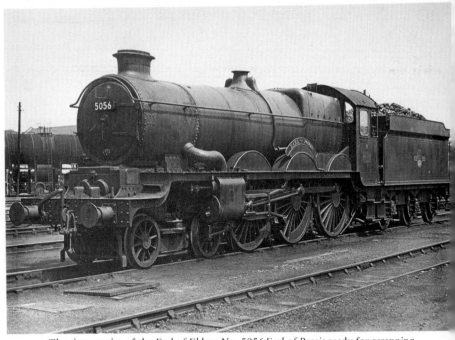

The sister engine of the *Earl of Eldon*, No. 5056 *Earl of Powis* ready for scrapping, with the number plates removed.

Author's collection

Bert Edmonds at Bristol Temple Meads with 'Castle' class No. 5097 *Sarum Castle*.

Author's collection

box, and produced from a bucket of water a two pint bottle of mother's lemonade, and handed it over to me. This was not like the wishy-washy gas filled products one can buy today, but neither was it anything like I had at home. It was cold, and the colour was a beautiful deep yellow. This lemonade had body, and like an old Port it had to be rolled around the mouth, and gently allowed to slide down the throat, leaving behind a thin skin on the teeth and a slight furring on the tongue, to be savoured for an hour afterwards. So I joined *Amyas* ready to enjoy the afternoon and learn how to fire a steam engine.

Amyas was nearing the end of her life and would not survive the year. She was run down, even at the low shunting speeds she knocked and clanked, and to draw ten coaches up out of the sidings produced more steam from the front end than reached her cylinders. The polished dome so glorious in the sunshine of her prime years, was now covered in several coats of paint, dirt streaked and greying, but even knowing she was to make her last journey in steam soon, was no excuse for footplate standards to fall where she was spotless.

Her cab boiler casing shone, countless rubbings with oiled cotton waste by numerous firemen had removed or thinned the original green paint through to the red of earlier years, the whole merging into a soft patchwork of colour. Her copper injector pipes were burnished into a warm light brown sheen, small hollows in the copper showing up clearly the evidence of many knocks she had received. The brass tank of her sight feed lubricator shone clean and smooth, the roughness of the casting polished away over the years of her long life. Even the brass strip on the screw reverser had been polished so many times the valve cut off marks were barely discernible. The regulator handle was smooth and warm in the hand, unhappily soon to rust away as the dampness and chill crept through her as she awaited the end at the place of her birth.

It was a wonderful afternoon. I was allowed to fire her, shaping the fire round the box, the back corners packed tight, the coal burning with a long curving flame, rolling under the brick arch then whipping up and over to lick against the tube plate as the draught from the open damper and fire box hole caught it. As the needle of the pressure gauge moved towards the blowing off mark I was shown how to work the live steam injector, and how this operation caused the water in the gauge glass to rise as the boiler filled. It was all so easy, I was at that stage of tender years not to know that the Passenger Pilot was one of the few undemanding duties for a fireman.

I was allowed to drive her back, light engine, into the spur, and to pull on the whistle chain with three short blasts when we were inside, clear of the main line points. I was then given a fistful of that multi-coloured cotton waste for my own use. I had arrived, and as I sat on the fireman's seat the 'Saints', 'Stars', and brand new 'Castles' would come striding out of the station, the enginemen looking down from their elevated footplates onto this poor worn out old lady but not with disdain, as they too had spent their fair share of time on her sisters. It was the special look of superiority of all main line crews pulling out of a station with a big four cylinder engine. They were the aristocrats of the main line, the big glamour boys, the 'hard hitters' working on the 'runners'. We were very much the small fry — we were seen, then promptly forgotten.

It was a feeling I would become very familiar with in later years, as we swept by on the main line, past some poor unfortunate colleague shunting out any of the goods yards of the small stations with the local 'pick-up'. No matter that perhaps yesterday we were engaged on the same duty. Today you saw them and that was all. A wave from their footplate might be acknowledged by a nod of one's head, or if in a charitable mood, we might reply by lifting a hand. That was an indication that all was well, the engine steaming freely, the coal first class and that we were at peace with the world. With a parting blast on the whistle we would be gone. If opposite was the case then there was a game to be played out, a deliberate piece of play acting, deception, cunning, call it what you might, but practised by all enginemen in the same situation when passing our mates on the 'pick-up'.

We could be in dire straights, running on the main line five minutes in front of a named express with 150 lb of steam on the pressure gauge, the water level bobbing in the bottom nut and the blower screwed as far as it would go. But honour would not allow our circumstances to be seen by our mates. If we had been seen in difficulties we would have been the subject of much ribald mess room talk. So the pricker would be placed back in the rack, the blower shut off and we would be sitting down so unconcerned for those vital few minutes as we passed to much whistle blowing. As soon as we were out of earshot, on would go the blower again and we would get stuck in, praying that the next distant signal would be at caution so that we could recover a little. A mile of running without the regulator open was a saviour, many, many times. The day was to come when I knew what main line superiority was all about.

Main line superiority started a long way from the main line. It began in the dark confines of the shed as a member of the cleaning gang. To become a fully blown member of a cleaning gang meant acceptance, and as in all industries where adventurous young men work in gangs, full membership meant that the initiation ceremony had to be carried out. It was short, not so sweet and not a bit like a wedding. In its way it was a very serious and memorable part of life, for it was one of the first steps towards manhood, sorting out the men from the boys. Some young lads would leave when their time drew near. It was too much to face because there was no help at hand, as firemen, drivers, foremen and shed staff kept well out of the way. The 'boy' was about to become a man, and when it was all over he would be addressed as an equal by all.

It began when walking into the cleaners' mess room on the Monday night at the start of the first night shift. When I look at that door next to the gents toilet at Didcot shed now, I still remember that first night. I walked in and as I did so the 15 watt bulb was switched out, and two smoking flickering flare lamps were lit, and the familiar mess room became at once the sacrificial chamber. I was lifted up by many hands, carried over and laid face up on the table, many hands then held me down while the senior cleaner began to pour a pint of heavy lubricator oil over me, my clothing having been removed. It was a ceremony that took place centuries ago, in fact it is mentioned in the Good Book, but not in the way this anointment was to take place. The senior cleaner climbed onto the shoulders of another cleaner who stood on a bench, and from a great height and with a leer on his face, with much concentration and deliberation he began to pour a pint of heavy lubricator oil all over one's most private possessions.

That oil came slurping out in a thick channel to narrow down with a pencil slimness as it spread. It would have been a help if they had warmed the oil. When it was all over their gentlemanly instincts came to the forefront. It was time for the cleansing ceremony; they all trooped out leaving the cleaning materials consisting of a bar of carbolic soap, a good stiff scrubbing brush, a quarter of a pint of paraffin, a handful of dry sand and a bucket of hot water, and, if you could clean the oil off with that, you could surely clean a locomotive. I can say from experience I did not attempt to ride my bike for a fortnight!

As a full blown cleaner one now took a step towards better things. I was no longer addressed as 'Boy', it became 'hey you' but although the anointment with oil was over there were two more tests to pass. One was to remove the foreman's bowler hat, the other to remove the chargehand cleaner from his cabin, without being caught.

With this in mind plans had to be made. As we were already on nights, target number one had to be the chargehand cleaner. Three methods had been tried with some success by previous lads. One could tie his cabin door to the door of the boilersmiths, then kick both doors and run, or one could lay cotton waste along the gap at the bottom of his door, set it smouldering and shout 'fire' after wedging it, or one could bung up his chimney with wet cotton waste and smoke him out.

There had to be another way and I found it. His stove was the standard type fitted in all the cabins. A cast iron pot bellied incinerator designed to burn good Welsh steam coal. The chimney was also cast iron with an elbow bend where it entered the top of the stove. This elbow was cast with a slot to take a damper, being a flat bit of iron that slid in and out as required to regulate the draught. By one o'clock in the morning that stove should be drawing well enough for the chargehand to push the damper in. He had allocated all the work, and had checked that we were all on the job, so, from his point of view it was reasonable for him to think he was safe to bed down for a couple of hours. Now if one was to take two fog detonators, straighten out the lead straps, make a bend at the end of the straps and tie on a long thread from the cotton waste, it should be possible to lower it carefully down the chimney and on to the top of the damper where a fog detonator would cook to perfection.

I climbed up the ladder and along the catwalk, counting the chimneys until I came to the right one before I carefully lowered the detonators. According to my calculations, explosives should go up, so he would be grateful to have his chimney cleaned, but, it never works out that way, the blast can go down. I climbed down from the roof and crept back to No. 6106 which was the engine I was cleaning and waited with the others for the bang. When it did come we were all disappointed, as there was no loud explosion, but just a dull thud as if someone had slammed a heavy door.

We waited, and his door opened to allow a large cloud of grey dust to come billowing out. It seemed to move towards a pannier tank, where it stopped, although there was some movement in the middle.

When the dust had settled a bit, it was just possible to see a figure coughing its lungs up onto the frame of the tank engine. It was Ernie Didcock our chargehand. He began to recover and get his breath back, and then I heard words I had never come across before, so all in all we had the impression that he was a little upset.

He got over it in time, but there were threats of us being sent home, and worst of all 'The Sack', but it blew over, as no real harm had come to him. The boilersmiths took him in, and Swindon stores van delivered a new stove three weeks later complete with a new damper. A month from the day, Reading sent two nice gentlemen to replace the window, repair the brickwork round the frame and put in new glass. It was never to be repeated, a cowl was fitted to that chimney and to my surprise and delight it is still there.

The second target, the foreman's bowler hat, had to be a day shift operation as the Boss did not work on nights. This duty was delegated to the shift foremen who only wore trilby hats and could be discounted. Also the shift foremen were drivers doing supervisory work who could go back to the footplate, and we could be sent to fire to them. There was no reason to stoke up trouble for the future. The Boss foreman was another matter. He was a much envied man who had the odd Saturday and every Sunday off.

As with the removal of the chargehand, there was a time honoured method of removing a bowler hat whilst it was being worn. A ball of wet cotton waste could be counted as a prime mover but it had several disadvantages, as one could miss and be caught. Therefore a new approach using basic scientific methods was called for, using two drawing pins from the notice board and a good strong length of thread from the cotton waste.

Bill Young our foreman was a man of habit, and his habit of inspecting his shed at dead on 9.00 a.m. was to be his undoing.

I was tightening up the dart handle on the smoke box of No. 3448 *Kingfisher* when he came out of his office. Bending down on the framing I was able to line up the height of the bowler with the door post. As soon as he was out of sight we went into action, the drawing pins were pressed into the woodwork, and the thread stretched tight across the doorway. We then awaited his return.

It was a long wait. We should have had sense to inspect the pit on Number 1 road opposite his office and call it off for another day, but young men do not possess any sense; they are thick, their heads are filled with solid bone, they are idle, good-for-nothing imbeciles with a total disregard for authority. Well, that's what he said on his return! We had forgotten to inspect the pit for water depth. As he walked through that doorway the thread whipped his bowler off, it bounced once, and landed in the pit, so quickly, that it was bobbing brim up in the sludge before he realised that it had been removed.

He stood there with his hands on his hips looking down into the pit. There was just enough sludge in the water to prevent a proper ripple. The displacement of the bowler was just enough to create a slight swell, but it proved the point, that bowler hats do float, and can be removed from heads by using science.

The recovery of the hat was another matter, the only scientific instrument at hand being a coal pick. A (kindly) fireman came to the rescue, hooking the spike end of the coal pick inside the rim, but by doing so caused the brim to tilt so that a little sludge slopped in. As the hat was lifted out the red silk lining became a porridge grey. The last engine on Number 1 road had received a boiler washout, so everything now had an explanation. As Bill took repossession his comments were unrepeatable. It was years afterwards I noticed that Bill had developed a habit when entering his office of always waving his arms about in front of him before entering. He did this even in the winter when all the wasps were gone and visiting enginemen put it down to Bill becoming slightly eccentric as he aged, but we knew different!

Cleaning locomotives did not end with their outsides. The tightening up of the dart handle of *Kingfisher* I described had been the end product of part of the inside cleaning, for I had been engaged in blowing tubes. The instrument provided for this operation was the steam lance, which was simple and effective, being a long piece of tubing tapered at one end to form a high pressure nozzle. The other end was clipped to a one inch flexible length of pipe, which in turn was coupled up with a union nut to the take-off valve from the main steam pipe of the stationary boiler. Alternatively it could be connected to the take-off valve of another engine that was in steam.

Every Great Western locomotive was equipped with this valve on the nearside of the smoke box. To control the steam lance a valve was fitted, and worked with a small lever. The procedure was to start at the bottom line of tubes, poke the nozzle end into a tube, pull the lever and blast the tube through, thus clearing it out. This should have been a straight forward operation, but one learned fast. It was advisable to wear cycle clips, tie string around the wrists to secure the sleeves, button up the overall jacket and pin it tight with a safety pin around the throat, jam the cap on, tie a handkerchief over the nose and mouth then crawl into the smoke box. The lance could now be used, and one hoped that the tube was clear, but if it was blocked then all the precautions taken were worthwhile. The back pressure would blast back high pressure steam to pepper one with cinders at high velocity.

When the dust had settled the old fashioned tube rod had to be used. This was a half inch steel rod, long enough to ram down the tube right through to the firebox. Once the tube had been rammed through, the lance could be used again, and so it went on, across the tube plate, a row at a time until all the tubes were clear.

The next stage of cleaning came at the other end, in the firebox, and that was an experience. Nine times out of ten the Driver booking defects had reported 'corks on tubeplate' so into the firebox we would go when it had been emptied, but with eighty odd pounds of steam pressure still in the boiler, it could be very hot.

The equipment provided was very simple, a sack, a handbrush, flare lamp, a short tube rod, a hammer, and most important of all, a coal pick. All the tools were laid out on the floorboards, the flare lamp was lit, the sack laid over the hot fire hole ring then you laid on your stomach, and slid feet first into the firebox. Next the tools were laid out on the brick arch, with the exception of the coal pick. This was insurance, for it was jammed in between the firebox doors to keep them open. It was not unknown for another cleaner to sneak up onto the footplate and close the doors with a parting remark of 'Let's see you get out of that, whack'.

Work could now begin. The clinker corks were clouted with the hammer, then the short tube rod used to clear up inside the tube. After each row had been dealt with it was time to stick your head out of the firebox for some cool air, and at the same time to half straighten the back, for it was impossible to stand up in a firebox. The whole operation had to be carried out in a crouching position.

Once the whole of the tube plate was clear it was brushed down, but by this time the brick arch was piled up with clinker and ash. Once again one found that the Great Western had provided the means for clearing the rubbish, for one brick had been left out in each far corner of the arch, so that all the muck could be brushed through onto the fire bars and into the ash pan.

On a summer day a hot firebox was not the place to hang about in, but in the winter it was a very desirable place. The cleaning would be completed, the sack pulled in and laid on the fire bars, then you could tuck yourself up in the back corner and have a quiet smoke. Now and again you would tap a stay with the hammer in case the chargehand was lurking about, for he knew from bitter experience that when cleaners go quiet something is wrong. The funny part about it all was that nobody wondered why winter fireboxes took longer to clean than summer ones, unless the foremen too could remember back to the days when they cleaned fireboxes.

Because of the labour shortage we sometimes had to act as fitter's mate. I had one month of that and it was enough. Two weeks were spent packing spindle glands on Pannier Tanks and 'Dean Goods' engines. It was not so bad sitting on the motion with the boiler casing pressing into the back of the neck, or using an enlarged cork-screw to pull out the old packing. The tricky bit came with packing in the new graphite twists, ramming them in with a thin blunt chisel, placing the gland back on the bolts, finding the thread for the nuts and lock nuts, then dropping one into the pit, and on recovering the nut, knocking the spanner back down while you were wriggling your way back up into the motion. It was during this period I learnt that the English language can be used in many brutal ways to express feelings, but worse was to come. After two weeks I was moved into the lifting shop to further my education.

Whenever I now go into the lifting shop at Didcot locomotive shed on their 'open days', I still remember that period of two weeks, and Churchward Mogul, No. 5379. She was in for attention to valves and pistons, and I was given the job of decarbonising the pistons, spending a week on each piston. I had carried out this job on my old A.J.S. motorcycle, and the instructions were clear in the hand book to use a soft scraper such as a flattened piece of solder, but on no account to use a screwdriver. It was a surprise to find that a steam engine collected carbon, and had such dirty great pistons, but it was a bigger surprise to be handed a whacking great lump hammer and a cold chisel large enough to complement this persuader.

The instructions were straightforward. You placed the chisel at an angle with the left hand against the piston head, and then belted that chisel with the right hand using the lump hammer to come into contact with the chisel head. This very sophisticated operation to remove carbon could be entrusted to any cleaner. At the first belt I expected to see carbon flying all over the place, but glancing up at the smirk on the fitter's face was an indication that it did not work out that way. I just made a small mark on the carbon, and the next blow produced a small chip of carbon flying off, just large enough to show the metal of the piston underneath. It was, I think, the most soul destroying job I have ever encountered. Hour after hour, small chips scattering onto the floor, and at the end of the day another four inch patch uncovered, and there was always the thought that the other piston was still waiting for my attention.

After cleaning both pistons my right shoulder ached from wielding that lump hammer, whilst my left hand was sore and bruised from the few times I had missed. So there and then I made a vow, that never again would a cleaner use that chisel. Now, after 30 years, it lies in my tool box, a reminder of the days when I learned many new words!

The prime objective of joining the Great Western locomotive department was to become an engine driver. It was possible even to become a foreman, but qualifications were required for that position. It was hinted, alleged, and darkly suggested that a certain number of stop blocks had to be knocked down before one could be considered for a foreman's job. Basic economics said it was cheaper to make a man up to foreman where he would not be able to drive locomotives and therefore knock down stop blocks. But, of course, this was all part of shed 'ribbing'. Before one could become a foreman or a driver, one had to become a fireman, and his main occupation was to work with a shovel. So far, except for filling the foreman's coal buckets, we had not been near a shovel. There was no training as such in the art of firing, as the Great Western had another method in introducing one to the shovel, in slow easy stages. One first had to prove that one could use a shovel, and in a busy locomotive shed there were so many types and shapes of shovels.

The first shovel to be placed in one's hands was a Number 8. This, on its own, was just another shovel. It had a shaft and a 'T' handle, nothing strange about that, it was just like dad's garden spade. It was at the other end where things began to go wrong. At that end any similarity to a garden spade ended, for this was a king size shovel. It had a great square blade big enough to lift half a hundredweight. It was a diabolical instrument, placed gently into your hand with a pat on the shoulder from the chargehand, and then he turned you in the general direction of the coal stage. At last, the unison between man, shovel and coal was to take place.

It was an exquisite moment to walk on to the coal stage, and to toss a coin as to who was to take the steel wagon against the wooden one. A ten tonner loomed high in the half light, so why toss to see which wagon to empty? They surely both held the same amount of coal, but alas, I still had a lot to learn. I drew the wooden one, knocked up the clips, and two tubs were filled as the coal came tumbling out. This was easy, nothing to it, until I slid the shovel in along the wagon bed, and I found the reason for tossing for the choice of wagon.

Wooden wagons were used for things other than the transportation of coal. The floor boards were uneven, and six inch nails had been inserted to secure items in transit with the last two inches of nail bent over in the process. As I slid that No. 8 shovel in as hard as I could the blade went under one of these nails. The shock wave went up the shaft, up my arm, and out at the elbow joint. I stood there stunned, and then the pain came. It was not a gentle pain, but a roaring rasping pain which left me trembling, gasping for breath, and, as in the lifting shop, added to my vocabulary.

When the last shovelful of coal was thrown out of that wagon I sighed with relief. The No. 8 shovel was now polished with not a trace of black paint to be seen on its once virgin blade. There were enough bent six inch nails in the floor boards to stock a shop. I borrowed a sledge hammer and belted those nails over and into the wood until they were flush, and felt a lot better for it.

After a period on the coal stage it was time to move on and be introduced to another type of shovel. If we were to become firemen we had to know how to throw coal into the firebox, but, we also had to know how to throw it out. Each engine carried such a shovel in case this had to be done out on the road, so we were led to the fire droppers' pit. Each engine as it came in had to be serviced, the fire had to be cleaned, or if the engine was in for a boiler washout the fire had to be thrown out completely. For this a special shovel was designed. It had a two foot square blade tied on to a twelve foot handle, all steel from end to end. It weighed enough to make one cough on the first attempt to lift it. To complement this tool was a steel bar, used to break up the clinker, and to complement the bar was a steel pricker, used to hook up the clinker so that the shovel could be used. With all this twelve foot long steelwork about, all that was needed was a cleaner eager to learn.

The Great Western had it all worked out. They allowed one hour to prepare the fire on a big engine, and three quarters of an hour for a small engine, so it stood to reason that the allowance for emptying the firebox was the same. But this did not always work out as planned, as an engine could be on the road for a long time, an empty tender would show that, and it could have burnt a load of poor coal. Engines would drop on to the ash road with the clinker up level with the fire hole ring, or, they could come off a train at short notice and arrive on the shed with a box full of fire, but either way they had to be cleaned out.

The only way to tackle this sort of job was to shovel all the fire to one side of the box, throw out the clinker, shovel the fire back over on the cleaned side, then throw out the clinker from the other side. It sounds simple enough, but lifting that twelve foot long shovel was no joke. It was red hot, so a heavy leather glove plus a pad of wet cotton waste had to be used by the left hand as the shovel was withdrawn from the firebox. With a tender engine it could be managed without much trouble, but on a tank engine it had its moments, enough to learn a few more words.

Once the firebox was clean, there remained only two more jobs to be carried out before the engine was moved forward to the coal stage. The ash pan and the smoke box had to be cleared, and it is a debatable point as to the merits of one to the other, because a lot depended on the wind. With the ash pan, both dampers were opened wide, and you climbed down into the pit with the ash rake. If the tender end was chosen then nine times out of ten the water scoop came into contact with the head. If the engine end was chosen the ramp could be missed by ducking lower only to clout the head on an axle. Whichever end one started there was always somewhere from which a drop of water would drip with uncanny accuracy onto the back of the neck.

With the rake in the hand it was now a question of pushing the ash to and fro until the ash pan was empty. With each push and pull the ash would cascade out of the pan, drifting up through the motion, up through the spokes of the driving wheels, and covering everything with a grey film of dust, including the poor lad responsible for this operation. The selection as to whether to start the tender end or engine end was arrived at by careful study of the wind direction. Obviously going in with the wind should have meant that the ash would be carried away, but again careful design in the building of the locomotive altered all calculations. The wind would drive under the engine, channelled through the pit to arrive at the ash pan as a gale, then it would eddy up round the boiler, whip round the smokebox, and come howling back down the pit to fill the air with dust. So at either end there was no escape. It was a matter of push and rake, head down, teeth gritted, until the job was finished and the dirty grey figure could climb out of the pit.

The last job was the smokebox. Again, depending on the state of the fire on the engine when she came in, and the amount of ash in the pan, one could guess on the amount in the smokebox. With a 'home' engine it would not be much, perhaps a foot deep, but with an engine that had been on the road for some time it could be up level with the locking bar, half way up the smokebox. One approached the smokebox door with a certain amount of caution, but for this operation there was no No. 8 shovel. By far the best tool was the fireman's shovel, so by devious steps we had almost reached our goal.

Hand over hand we would proceed along the top framing to the smokebox. Knocking up the locking handle and unscrewing it a couple of turns, giving the dart handle a quarter of a turn and pull. The smokebox door would then swing sweetly open to allow half a hundred weight of black cinders to slide out and cover one's boots. This was first shovelled off the front framing, then one could begin to shovel it out of the smokebox onto the ground, and, as with the ash pan, the wind would whip round the smokebox door, and try to blow it all back in again! But endeavour must prevail. The smokebox door would be swung round and closed, enabling her to go forward for coaling.

All this effort had produced a clean firebox, smokebox and ash-pan, with an engine all ready to be prepared for the road once again, but it had left behind a pit full of ash, a pile of clinker, and a heap of cinders. Whilst one was in the pit shovelling out the ash, the forward planning of the Great Western came into being. Without the aid of computers, measured day work, slide rules or gentlemen in white coats consulting stop watches, somehow the wagons one emptied on the coal stage had made their way down the bank, and arranged themselves in a long line on the ash road siding, all ready to be filled with the cinders, ash and clinker. Once again the No. 8 shovel was picked up and used as it was designed to be, and so, one was introduced to the shovel and its variants.

It was good basic training and at the same time using that training to advantage, for when the time came to use the fireman's shovel, it was an old friend. It had a handle attached to a long narrow blade and with it one could twist the wrist, flick, turn, slide, and place the coal just where it was required — it was a beautiful tool. In addition one could wash the hands in it, and bacon and eggs fried in it were far superior to those cooked in any frying pan on the market. That fireman's shovel was just one of the small parts that went into making the Western 'Great'.

On a recent visit to the Torbay Steam Railway I was met with a very pleasant surprise on entering the reception hall of Queens Park Station at Paignton. For there, hanging in a place of honour on the wall was a fireman's shovel, which drew me with affection. The posters and the book shop were forgotten, for here was the instrument responsible for all the successes of the great record breaking runs. Yet the people gathering round No. 4588, the beautiful little tank engine that had just arrived, ignored the shovel on the wall.

I had, over the years, used the shovels of all the other companies but they were heavy and narrow and quite devoid of any character. To the ordinary person it might seem stupid to talk of a shovel in such a way, but then, steam enthusiasts are supposed to be a race apart. The Great Western shovel was a fitting companion to a Great Western locomotive, balanced to perfection, it completed the unison between fireman and firebox. The only thing I could never understand, along with every other fireman, was, how that firebox grew in size once a fire was in it.

I knew from cleaning days that it was not possible to stand up inside a firebox, and yet once that fire had been built up and the locomotive was being used to pull 500 odd tons that firebox assumed gigantic proportions. It became a raging furnace, its demands for fuel only met by a brother to that shovel hanging on that wall at Paignton. Without a doubt it was a fitting gesture, and the mark of 'someone who cared', to hang it there.

A book on Great Western engine working would not be complete without a few pages devoted to a band of ladies who were to be found all over the system where crossroads meet. In their way they helped to make the Western 'Great' for they provided the 'Double Home' lodge.

In my day as a fireman the 'change-over en route' put an end to lodging between shifts, but I knew of these ladies. There was one in Old Didcot, Mrs. Kate Bennett, who provided such a service for men from Severn Tunnel Junction shed, Wolverhampton and Westbury. I would look at these strange men dressed in enginemen's uniform, and wonder with a small boy's mind, how could there be other men wearing the same clothes as my dad? To me in those days the Great Western began and ended at Didcot. Looking back now, what on earth could they do in such a small place except go for a walk, or go to the pub?

Father, I knew, went to a far off town called 'Brumigum', where there was a place called the Bull Ring. He would bring back large brown paper bags filled with all kinds of biscuits, and sweets of every colour not to be found in the village shops. This 'Brumigum' was a wonderful place. I knew too that he stopped with a lady called Annie but it was years later that I found that Birmingham was not a fairyland, and from what he told me about Annie and the 'Double Home' lodge, it was not a high class hotel.

All the Didcot men lodged with Annie, in a little terrace house tucked away in the maze of streets, later to be swept away, with the old Bull Ring, in a holocaust of fire and destruction as aerial warfare rained high explosives and incendiary bombs into those little back yards. I never met Annie, but from what I heard of her she was a kindly soul, cooking meals and providing beds in what must have been very difficult circumstances with a 24 hour turn-over of enginemen. This turnover created problems for it was common practice to arrive in the early hours, light a candle, then after a wash, creep up to bed to find that another was just leaving it. The bed, of course, did not have time to cool and if the needs of nature called, a groping hand under the bed would locate the required receptacle, and, in the gloom the reward for this discovery was often a wet thumb. Neither father nor his mate ever did explain how they emptied that pot, except that it was advisable to hide one's boots!

Meals were taken in the kitchen, a table being pushed up to a window overlooking a small back yard, but this window always had the bottom half slightly open for the benefit of the cat. Annie in this respect was typical of her generation. Home was not complete without a cat, but where other ladies enjoyed the company of an ordinary cat, Annie owned a tiger, a whacking great ginger tom, whose sole delight was to jump through the window and land on the table. He then would walk down the middle with great confidence, secure in the knowledge that with Annie there he would come to no harm.

He would pick his way delicately through the plates, sniffing at some morsel of delicious sausage, his tail straight up, while all around him were a lot of rough, uncouth enginemen, knives and forks poised, with one eye on his progress and one eye on Annie. He had the luck of the Devil, as plans to stop this parade were laid and thwarted, for Annie was always there. When his end did come it was just as swift, without the aid of planning, a combination of luck and circumstances, plus quick thinking by two men. Quick thinking to deal with an emergency was part and parcel of footplate life. Ginger was up against the experts, and as expected, those experts acted instinctively.

Ginger as usual came through the window, landed on the table, and began his parade to the other end. He was not to know that on this day, the Insurance man was due to call. The brass knocker was lifted to 'rat-a-tat' on the front door, the echo rebounding up the passage in a hollow boom. Annie got up from her chair and padded up the hallway to answer the call, and with her movement the experts went into action.

Ginger had begun his journey back up the table, his tail still upright and weaving from side to side, but as Annie's slippers were heard, slapping their way up the passage towards the dining room, the escape route was quickly cut off and the window closed. A Birkenhead fireman who was just about to spread some mustard on his sausage, changed the direction of the knife and very gently wiped it on the exposed backside of Ginger. Only a fireman used to the delicate setting of an exhaust injector could have used such finesse. So gentle was the touch of the knife that Ginger took two more steps forward before coming to a sudden stop. Then he extended his claws and stood on tiptoe, his back arched up and his fur stood out like stiff golden wire. There was a long low whistle as the air expended from his lungs. He came back on his hindquarters as his muscles stood out, then with one almighty leap he was gone, straight through the closed window.

Ginger never came back, perhaps he headed for the canal. Anyway, Annie was not without a cat for long. The same fireman brought her a little black kitten on his next trip, and that kitten knew its place. It never came near a table or a mustard pot.

Chapter Three

Footplate work was a life rich in incidents, no working day was the same, that was the beauty of it. As a boy I was enthralled by the stories of engines and drivers that my dad encountered. One in particular concerned driver Arthur Timms. He and his wife were a wonderful couple, they were more like an Uncle and Aunt to me. Their bitch had given me the little dog that was my constant companion, so when he trotted off home to see his mum each day it was natural that I should follow him. Besides, Mrs. Timms kept a secret store of sweets, and she was glad of the company of a small boy when Arthur and dad were away.

On one occasion they had gone off to 'Brum' in the early hours, and for some reason the return working was cancelled, so they were sent home as passengers. Even in my day as a fireman this was a rare treat. To be able to relax on the 'cushions', feel the slight snatch of the train, and see the smoke drifting over the fields, and know that for once another fireman was hard at work providing the power to let one laze back half asleep. There was one drawback to this short lived Utopia, the travelling public, the fare paying passengers.

Enginemen travelling home on the 'cushions' are a clannish lot. They would be the first to admit that the public had every right to a seat in a compartment, but any interference with the privacy of 'overalls, steam talk and railway work' meant that the fare payer was to some extent an interloper, to be removed with all possible speed. In the competitive world the steps taken would be classed as tactics, but in fairness, it was only used against city gents. Ladies, children and vicars were all made welcome.

Arthur arrived back home with father, and related, to his wife's outraged indignation, how he had removed a compartment full of city gents in a most expert manner. I can remember the story almost word for word, not only for its simplicity, but because it was such a laugh to hear.

They had left the train in the yard at Birmingham and taken the engine on light to Wolverhampton, where they were instructed to return home. As the next Up train started from this point they were able to secure a compartment to themselves long before departure time. As departure time drew near, more and more people squeezed in, and Arthur found that his ample proportions were subject to some restriction.

As this was a local train it was all non-corridor stock, so, whoever got in was stuck there until the next station was reached. There were some disdainful sniffs and glances of disapproval from these office types at having to share a compartment with two dirty old enginemen, so Arthur began to implement a plan of removal. As he said later, he had fired the old 'Dean Singles' and 'Armstrongs' up and down this stretch of line years before some of these lads had been born, and now, in his mature years, he was entitled to spread himself out a bit and enjoy the ride. It was to be a two stage operation, to remove a few at the next stop, and the remainder before they reached Birmingham, using two weapons, one for each stage.

Arthur was well built and sported a large corporation. With the greasy old cloth cap he wore, his image did not complement the white collars and bowler hats around him. Under his shirt he had been blessed by nature, with a chest full of hair, so when he carefully, and with deliberation, began to undo his shirt buttons and exposed all that masculinity, there was a slight easing of the pressure, and when he placed his hand in that luxurious growth and began to dig deep there was a distinct shuffle-up. He was still scratching away, a look of exquisite pleasure on his face as the train ran into Wednesbury station. Four passengers made a quick exit, but six remained huddled up in one corner, so stage two would have to be used.

In common with most footplate men, Arthur, besides being an expert driver was an expert at growing flowers or vegetables. In common with these experts, he specialised, and his speciality was onions. The onions he grew were not ordinary onions for pickling or cooking, but magnificent onions, as big as cricket balls and as solid, with a bite that made a Bombay curry taste like custard. So when Arthur stood up, and lifted his wicker basket down from the luggage rack, and took out one of these onions there was a slight stirring at the other end of the compartment.

To show that he was a gentleman and familiar with the finer points of etiquette, Arthur laid a napkin on his lap, searched around in his pockets, and produced a knife, a knife honed down to the sharpness of a scalpel. The operation then took place, with

45

all the artistry of a showman and the skill of a surgeon. The knife slid in and removed layer upon layer of dry skin, until the onion lay naked and glistening on his lap.

As a rabbit watches a stoat so did the remaining passengers watch this performance. Papers were laid on knees and forgotten, and eyes peered over the tops of spectacles. One passenger had an unlit cigarette between his lips, and a burnt out match between forefinger and thumb. Then Arthur delivered the *coup de grâce*, biting into that onion he began to scrunch. It was merciful at this point that the train was running into West Bromwich. The exodus began before the coaches had stopped, indeed, the actual stopping slammed the door shut behind them. Arthur leaned over, picked up an abandoned newspaper and settled back to enjoy a good read while he finished his 'fruit'.

As an example of a wicked bit of skulduggery it was a classic, designed to completely demoralise the opposition, and in their way most enginemen could equal it. This removal of passengers was also practised during my firing days. One of my drivers, dear old Bill Champ, went into battle with a most evil smelling pipe, that gurgled and made little popping sounds when he sucked on it, the smoke emerging from his mouth as a yellow-grey fog, while that curling up from the bowl was blue tinged and smelt of old drains.

Ted Hurle my regular mate for so many years could develop a twitch to discourage any interloper, being able to move his left shoulder, eye and nostril all in one movement. My old dad could produce the most body shaking, wracking cough imaginable, but, as I have written before, we were not entirely devoid of good manners. Room, conversation, and entertainment were always provided for ladies, children and vicars. In later years however, Management provided a reserved compartment next to the engine for its train crews. It was very considerate of them, but it was, at the same time, a two-edged sword, an insurance to cover any eventuality that might happen on the footplate ahead of us.

We loco-men at Didcot were lucky in one respect. Our duties were not confined to the main line, and the branch, in our case the Didcot, Newbury, Winchester and Southampton line, was typical of most branches. It was so divorced from the main line as to become a separate railway, and we knew all the stations' staff and their families, the plate-layers and signalmen, the farmers and coal merchants. We watched with interest the growth of wheat and cattle and the progress of ploughing and hedge trimming. We knew

46

the branch as well as our own back yard, even the passengers became friends, for we took the children to school, father to work, and mother into Newbury on market day.

The tenders of 'Dukes', 'Dean Goods', Collett 22XX's and 'Bulldogs' were built not only to store coal and water for the firebox and boiler, but to transport bean rods, pea sticks, sacks of potatoes, and young fruit trees. On Mondays, which as every male knows is wash day, and a good day to be at work, station masters' ladies would appear from station houses with two empty buckets. They stood opposite the footplate as we ran into the station. They knew from long experience that the injector would be on, and from that little curly pipe came boiling hot soft water. If by chance the coal bucket also stood there empty, then it was quickly filled.

One gentleman we took good care of was the brother of the beloved Dick Shepherd of St. Martin in the Field, for he had sustained the most awful injury to his neck. He was tightly strapped up, for the slightest jerk could endanger his life, and yet, in spite of this drawback he was the most cheerful of men. We would collect him at Newbury and take him through to Whitchurch, making each station stop in between on the hand brake and just a whiff of vacuum, stopping and starting so gently so that there was no possible chance of the coupling snatching.

Out in the sections, miles from civilisation, the platelayers would hold up an empty bucket, or go through a charade of warming hands in front of a fire. If there was time, a large lump of coal would be quickly thrown over the side, enough to keep them happy for a few hours, for they knew that on the return run we would remember them. The running plate would be stacked up with half a dozen large lumps, and they would be waiting, spread out over a quarter of a mile of the section, as the coal came tumbling over the side, one piece at a time, like large bombs leaving an aircraft. But it was not a one way traffic. The next day as we ran into the station, a ganger would be waiting with a couple of rabbits ready for skinning, and sometimes a couple of cock pheasants. Once, only once, we ran down a young deer between Woodhay and Highclere. We left a message with the signalman as to the exact location of a free dinner and the next day we collected a hind quarter as we ran in. We would help load a stubborn calf into the guard's van; a poor little bewildered animal, his head, tail and legs sticking out of a sack. Sometimes if the back end was clean, it was easier to pick him up and carry him in, bawling his head off and covering us with slobber as only a calf can. We would give an excited school boy a ride between stations, to see in that boy a mirror image of oneself only a few short years before.

Only once can I remember baulking at helping to unload live-stock from a guard's van. We ran into Compton and found our two minutes station time extended. I had seen the porter go into the van, but the minutes ticked away with no sign of him or the guard coming out, so I climbed off the footplate and walked back up the platform. When I reached the van and looked in I found both the guard and the porter pinned up at the end of the assortment of milk churns, trunks, crates of live chickens and other miscellaneous items of branch line revenue, by one very angry, large, billy goat. He had somehow managed to jump the link of what had been a short chain over the hook, so that the short chain became a long one, sufficient to cut off any chance of escape through the door.

Billy stood there, head down, pawing the van floor, breathing fire and thunder, his curved horns aimed at a point, level with our guard's navel. They were very frightened railway employees and there was nothing in the Rule Book to cover this situation. I told them to stop where they were while I went and enlisted help. It was a silly thing to say, as they were not going anywhere, but it was all I could think to offer for comfort. I ran back to Ted Hurle and explained the situation to him.

As always he had an answer to this problem, but then, as a fireman, he had worked the Welsh Valleys, where the transportation of Welsh mountain rams was commonplace. A bit of local knowledge was called for, far removed from the ideas that went into writing a Rule Book. He told me to go back to the van and tell both men to hang on as he was going to knock the billy goat off his feet. When the opportunity arose they were to run clear.

I passed this information on, wondering just what Ted intended to do. However, he had the tool to perform with, our engine, the little 'Collett' No. 2222, renowned for her quick acceleration. Ted blew off the brakes and opened her up. Her chimney blasted her up the platform the length of one coach, then Ted slapped on the anchors and almost stood her on her nose. That poor old billy goat went up to the other end of his chain with a thump, and at the same time the porter and our guard dived out of the door. At Newbury, it took four porters, two with shunting poles, to unload that goat. He bucked and kicked his way all up the platform, scattering waiting passengers in all directions, until he reached the exit. Here he became as docile as a lamb, for the station foreman had thrown the water out of the fire bucket over him. Here was one more railwayman who had met this situation before.

There was one occasion when we collected an unusual passenger at Churn Halt. This little platform was unstaffed and miles from anywhere. It was perched on top of the Berkshire Downs between Upton and Compton. If we had any passengers to drop there, the Guard would inform us, either at Didcot or Newbury. So far as passengers to pick up were concerned, we would slow down and stop if it was necessary, but it was not often that we did have a passenger to collect. These rare occasions were only in the summer when the odd rambler or a marksman from the rifle range required transport, but on this particular day, running to Newbury as light engine, we spotted a small white bundle on the platform. We stopped to investigate, and there curled up into a ball was one very lonely lamb.

At first we thought it was dead and had been abandoned as the Downs were usually covered with sheep. But not today, as they had all moved on leaving this one hungry and frightened lamb. There was only one thing to do. I picked him up, cuddled him in my arms, and took him back on to the footplate. We dropped him off at Compton into the loving arms of the station master's wife, where he settled down to become the family pet.

Churn Halt had another attraction at certain times of the year. In the fields nearby were to be found the most delicious button mushrooms, and during the mushroom season, light engines and the local goods would move about between sections, a little more smartly than usual, so that a quick stop could be made. Even before the engine or train had come to a stand, either the driver or fireman was shinning down the steps from the footplate to hop over the fence, cap in hand, to get picking. There was no need to look round as you stood where you landed, and picked them around you, five minutes being long enough to fill a cap to the brim. Sometimes we must have been just a little longer than five minutes, but never did the signalmen at Upton or Compton carry out Regulation 11, 'Train unusually long time in the section', as set out in the General Appendix to the Rule Book, perhaps because we shared our good fortune with them.

The branch, either side of Newbury, was like our own back yard. We knew it upside down and inside out, because most of the Didcot drivers had fired over it for so many years, and as my Ted had been up and down the Welsh valleys for so long, this switchback road held no terrors for him. We ran everything that could be thrown at us without any incidents, although there were a few near squeaks. Whitchurch was one of the worst places on the down road. After leaving Burghclere there was a little climb for about half a mile, then a little piece of flat about the length of a goods train, followed by the drop down to the other side of Whitchurch, like falling over a cliff.

We had a set pattern on this section of the branch, born from long experience. As soon as the engine dipped her nose down that bank, we would screw the tender handbrake down, and join all the buffers of the wagons up together. Sweeping down through Litchfield, we should have them in hand, enough perhaps to give the engine a little steam. There followed a very short section of rising gradient, but once over this, it was a matter of screwing another half a turn on the handbrake each time the driver gave her a burst of vacuum, and that way, we could drop down to Whitchurch with the train well under control. The protection for the Up road, was just outside the signal box in the form of a pair of throw off points that could land one in the road below. It was a fearsome place, and many a time we were ready to bail out, particularly in thick fog, but somehow we always managed to stop in time.

It was with regret that we lost all this lovely section of the branch to the Southern Region on 2nd April 1950. The rolling Hampshire Downs would be sadly missed, as Enborne Junction onwards became the territory of the Eastleigh lads. It was a fair swop in a way as we had been running into Eastleigh and Southampton for years, but we felt some concern for them as we knew just what that part of the branch was like. It was no place for the unwary, and it was not long before the first nasty incident occurred.

On 23rd September 1950, a B.R. 'Mogul' No. 76017, was working the 7.0 a.m. from Banbury to Eastleigh freight, and its driver lost control of the train on the bank down into Whitchurch. I can only imagine the awful moments on that footplate when its crew realised that the train was out of control. I've had it happen once, and the feeling of utter helplessness is a thing I would not wish on anyone. The crew got away with their lives by leaving her, jumping, as she ran through the catch points and buried her nose halfway down the bank before rolling over, leaving the remains of six wagons spread all over the place.

The steam crane came from Eastleigh to the rescue with the breakdown gang: Bill Bishop was the driver of the crane, and when it came to dealing with this sort of incident he was the top man to have on the job. It was not an easy lift, they never were. No. 76017 had to be brought half way over, and propped up, to stop her sinking, before Bill could lift her right out and place her back onto the rails.

Three months went by and the branch settled down. Then early one morning, Bill was again called out of bed. Another lad had landed down the bank at Whitchurch in a carbon copy of the first derailment, and one that gave as much trouble as the first. But this time Bill knew the snags. She was lifted out, and Bill went back to bed two days later! Another three months passed, and just as Bill was going out one evening, a messenger from Eastleigh shed caught him with the news that there was an engine buried in the earth outside Whitchurch box. Three times in a row! Bill thought that perhaps he had better get a paint pot and brush out, and paint little engines on the cab of his steam crane. The score was beginning to mount, but when Bill did lift this one out it was to be the last. The Eastleigh lads had learned the hard way.

During the winter months, of course, the branch could be a hell hole. As long as we kept running we were the sole means of communication between the villages that were strung out across the Downs to Newbury and Winchester. In the early days of the branch, there had been a period when trains had been snowed in for days but a lesson had been learned from this. In bad weather the shift foreman would send a light engine over to keep the cuttings clear of drifts, and it could be a hairy journey at times. The wind would drive the snow up into those forty foot deep cuttings, carving and shaping the ice into a beautiful sculpture, all up the face of the chalk cliff, where it hung in a glistening sugar overhang. Then as we passed the blast from the chimney would bring great sections of ice down where it would be crushed, powdered, and flung out from beneath the wheels, filling the cutting with a swirling fog of ice dust.

Clawing our way up with a heavy train, we must have looked like some forbidding prehistoric monster with our front buffer beam, vacuum pipe and cylinders covered with caked snow, whilst above the round black smoke box, our chimney erupted a vast column of escaping smoke and steam. Above it all, raged the white wall of a blizzard sweeping over the top of the cutting, and without warning the sanctuary of the iced cliffs would suddenly drop away and we would be out into the weather, and the bleak desolation of the Berkshire Downs. The snow drove into the cab, to spit and hiss as it touched the firebox flap. The lovely green fields and gentle rolling Downs were transformed into an English Siberia. It was as if nothing lived in this wasteland except this black monster with its line of snow covered wagons snaking across the tundra, leaving a trail of smut and ash to mark its passing.

In July 1974, almost ten years after the closure of the branch, and twenty years after I had last worked over it, I took a day off from factory life and returned, making a start at Upton station. Here I intended to stand on the road bridge to take some photographs, but as I drove my car towards the station I could see that my carefully laid plans were to fall through. The dual carriageway road on which I was driving had been formed by blowing up the station bridge and allowing it to fall into the cutting.

I turned off what once had been a quiet country road, into the station yard, parked, and sat there quietly looking round. The station house, in outline, was much the same as I had remembered it. To the right was the small cattle pen and goods yard. The goods shed was still perched on its small island platform, while across the remains of the yard, the coal merchants platforms were beginning to crumble, standing in isolation beside an empty trackbed.

As I left the car, and walked towards the station house to find out if it was permissible to explore my dear old branch, it was with delight and surprise that I found the occupant was one of my old mates from the days of cleaning and firing, Mick Slade, still on the footplate as a diesel driver. Mick, like myself, had blasted through this very station, shovelling his way up from Didcot, and up the banks I was soon to walk. Any talk of steam was quickly dispelled by Mick with the swiftness of a douche of cold water. He was now firmly a diesel man, glad that steam had gone for ever, and considered that anyone who hankered after the return of steam was quite mad.

I took stock of his surroundings. The platforms were empty and forlorn, grass covered, the edging slabs beginning to lift. On the Up side, clinging precariously to the rotting wooden fence, and struggling to survive, was a solitary rambler rose, the last red splash of beauty that used to stretch the entire length of the platform. The empty trackbed and embankment stretched away towards Didcot, twisting and curving through the fields, like the bony spine of some long dead monster. I turned south, and began to trudge up the 1 in 106 climb to the summit, leaving the roof of that sad station, slipping from view.

Past the first small cutting, the old railway flattened out into an undergrowth of thistles and young saplings. The tangled remains of the old Starter and Outer Home signal wires, running through pulleys wrenched out of foundation blocks, threaded their way forward to disappear in a wilderness of new growth. Two young heifers gazed at me, impassionately, through a gap in the hedge, not knowing that their grandmothers would have fled from the sound of open cylinder drain cocks from a 'twenty-eight', pounding up this bank.

At the start of the next cutting, I came across the body shell and stripped remains of an old Morris Minor car crouching amongst the nettles. A reminder of this 'throw away' world. I was then into the bank, deep chalk cliffs on either side, the remains of the platelayers huts standing drunkenly in a recess of the cutting, the concrete bins still full of small chippings, no longer required to be packed underneath the few odd sleepers rotting in the grass.

The memories came flooding back as I turned the next curve and came to the first overbridge, with its brickwork still showing the black stain of smoke from the countless chimneys that had punched their way through. The soot now was beginning to peel, revealing the brickwork to the sun and the rain for the first time in sixty years. It was all so peaceful and quiet now. The clink of the platelayer's shovel had given way to the whispering wind in the undergrowth. The sharp crisp 'bark' of a Collett 'twenty-two', scampering eagerly along, was now replaced with the noise of chalk fragments, as a rabbit scrambled frantically up the cliff face. The heavy rumble of the big American 'Baldwin', Class 8F 'Staniers', and Churchward 'twenty-eights', clawing their way, yard by yard, up this incline, was now reflected by the distant groaning of a tractor working in the fields high above.

I came across a barrier of rails, bolted into uprights sunk deep into the old trackbed. I climbed over and round the next curve, plodding on, breathing heavily with the climb. Then, just as I remembered, stood the three arch bridge, tall, striding, over the 40 feet high cutting, towering over me, the centre arch framing the blue sky and billowing white clouds. I brushed my way through the undergrowth and sat down under the bridge, my back up against the brickwork.

I closed my eyes and drifted back, to the days when this bridge had meant the halfway mark going up, and 'nearly home' on the way down. I could see it, sliding into view through the eyeglass as we pounded our way up, a tall, gaunt, three legged bridge, that seemed to be looking down at us contemptuously from its lofty height. The arches were far too high to be a target for our blasting exhaust, and on the return journey it would assume the proportions of a model, as we swung round the curve and down into the bank, three thin legs spanning a deep gorge. We would then swoop down, rushing through with the wind, as if escaping from its clutches.

I opened my eyes to see a baby rabbit sitting on the other side of the bank, ears up, and nose twitching, as he pondered over this stranger. As I moved to stand up, he turned and bounded away, tumbling over something in the tall grass. I crossed over and found the reason for his tumble as he scampered up the bank. Lying in the tall grass, was a firebar. How long had it lain there, and from which engine had it come? I left it there in peace.

I turned away a little sad, and made my way on up the bank, and as I rounded the curve, an hour out from Upton, I found the way blocked. This time the cutting was not filled with a deep drift of snow but with bales of straw, right up, level with the ridge. Four tarpaulins stretched across to form a roof. An ingenious farmer had found the perfect way to store his winter feed.

As I was determined to reach the top of the bank, I climbed over and carried on, through the last bridge, and to the top of the Downs. The last few hundred yards caused me some concern, as it had become a dumping ground or storage place, for farmyard manure, and as such, was in the process of maturing. Finding a flat piece of wood, I skirted the worst of the manure with great difficulty, using the wood to form a platform, and to clean my boots afterwards. From there, it was clear going to Churn.

As I left the bank behind, the trackbed stretched out ahead, the only sign of its path being the remains of the fencing on either side. The grass had grown tall, bending over where I passed through, and at last I came to the site of Churn Halt, with the goods shed of Compton just showing in the distance. There my nostalgic ramble had to end as there was no time to go further. I turned and saw my tracks in the grass leading from the top of the bank; I must have been the first mortal to pass this way for a long time.

It really came home to me, my dear old branch was dead, sleeping peacefully along with Grimm's Ditch and the old Roman encampments. In 1882 the first steam shovel had ripped this gigantic trench out of the Berkshire Downs, exposing the white chalk in an ugly scar across the countryside. Wagonloads of spoil had backed down behind the shovel to be tipped at Upton following down into Didcot so by building up the embankment.

Thousands of people had been conveyed along this old railway along with countless thousands of tons of material, generations of locomotives from the little Metro tanks to the big 2-8-0 freights had been a pageant of development pounding up this bank together with generations of enginemen, myself amongst them.

The older generation have long passed on together with the steam locomotive, they had built it and worked it, now they were dead and the branch with them, but together they had fitted into the vast jigsaw pattern of the Great Western Railway.

I made my way back down the bank towards Upton. I knew that under the grass, rippling so gracefully in the gentle breeze, the trackbed was still there, wending its empty way right through to Newbury, and onwards from Enborne Junction, it continued across the Hampshire Downs into Winchester. Its scars were covered and softened with grass and chickweed, thistles and nettles. My branch had returned to the peacefulness of nature.

A skylark rose under my feet and climbed up into the blue summer sky, its shrill whistling growing fainter as it gained height. Then the agony of it all hit me, here were the remains of a perfectly good railway, a direct link between the Midland factories and the docks at Southampton. Yet for almost its entire length, the road ran alongside, choked up with continental lorries, snarling their way up inclines. Forty lorries equalled the loads we pounded up the same incline with one steam locomotive.

It was a sad walk back down that bank. My movements would flush out a pair of wood pigeons bursting out from a thicket, with frantic flapping of wings, leaving a trail of small feathers to float down into the grass, and pheasants squawked with indignation, as they scurried out of my way, the sudden noise as startling to me as it was to them. Rabbits scampered along in front of me, dodging from side to side in their haste to escape from a lonely sad man, who could remember another generation of rabbits who ran with the wind, ahead of a steam locomotive charging at them through this deep cutting.

I sat in my car at Upton station, and changed out of my heavy boots. The enormity of my nostalgic visit was too much to take in and retain perspective. I had even forgotten to use my camera. Then the thought struck me that I could return, it would still be there, and this time I would be prepared.

Nostalgia is a state of mind, of regret and reproach, sadness and disillusion, and it can slice deep into one with intensity. It is a personal emotional feeling that can be dismissed as a weakness, to be tossed aside by those who do not experience such feelings. It is said that one should never look back, never return, but from nostalgia can come memories, and from those memories, and the foresight of a few who used their cameras, the branch can live again. Once more the 'Castles' can march proudly out of Paddington, and slide swiftly under the lee of Dawlish cliffs, and the big 'twenty-eights' can again pound their way up the very bank I had just descended.

There are men like myself who can remember, and men like my dear old Uncle, Bert Edmonds of Old Oak Common, now in the winter of his life, and who I must turn to, and perhaps rekindle the memories of the 'Limited', 'Bristolian', the 'Red Dragon' and the 'Cheltenham Flyer'.

Chapter Four

A good example of what Bert Edmonds was like on the foot-plate can best be described from his, and others' recollections of a particular run related to me. He was working one of the Up Swansea expresses with No. 5027 *Farleigh Castle*, an Old Oak Common engine and one that he was familiar with, and as it turned out it was a good job he knew her.

She was in a bad way, leaking steam where she should be tight and riding badly on her boxes, but steamwise she would hold her own with a good fireman. And that was part of the trouble. Through circumstances since forgotten, Bert had with him a spare fireman, a lad who was eager enough but who did not have any experience with big passenger engines or fast running. He could only do his best.

Bert nursed *Farleigh Castle* as much as he could without losing time, but when he ran into Cardiff, the blower was on to keep the pressure up and he had half a glass of water showing in the gauge. They could manage to Newport but it was the voice on the station tannoy that confirmed his fears; "Newport, next stop, then fast to Paddington". Now Bert was not a praying man, well, not on the footplate anyway. It is true the Lord looks after His own, but in this case he needed some help, and it came with the arrival of an old workmate, driver Fred Nash.

Fred was in the process of learning the road between Paddington and South Wales, both ways, and he was now on his last trip back to the 'Smoke' before signing the book and taking his place in the Link. He was a very welcome addition for the long run home, and Bert explained the position to him knowing full well that his fellow driver would get stuck in, should the need arise.

The short run to Newport was made without any trouble, but that was just a lull before the coming storm. They had hardly come to a stand at the end of the platform before another member of Old Oak Common shed climbed aboard, in the form of Locomotive Inspector George Price. He was an old friend to both Bert and Fred, as they had gone through the mill from cleaner to driver together. Bert thought that he had joined them for the ride home and to check out the young fireman who, with good reason, looked scared stiff. He was working under the eyes of two senior drivers and now an inspector, but his fears were groundless. George Price had not come to see him at work. It was the two 'Royals' they were tacking on to the 'back end' that George was concerned about.

Bert was dumbfounded, as any Royal train working was unheard of without the driver and fireman being specially picked, and with a locomotive in first class order. Somewhere there had been a slip up, but the two Royal coaches were there, and the Great Western had to get them home.

George wanted Bert to have a 'banker' as far as Badminton, but as he explained, he had just his full load and no way would he suffer the indignity of having a tow, even if the engine was rough and fired by a young lad. Bert had plans up his sleeve, cemented by the arrival of Fred Nash back at Newport. Poor old George Price was not happy about this situation at all, and little did he know what was in store.

It was Bert's habit, when with his regular fireman, to do at least 60 miles of firing each day. It was a fourfold arrangement and one that endeared him to all of his firemen mates. It gave the fireman a rest, and a taste of driving a big passenger engine. Bert kept his hand in with the shovel, and as he explained to me, it kept him fit.

For a man in his sixties that was a bit of an understatement, as Bert was as fit as any of his firemen. He asked very politely if George would stand up in the fireman's corner out of the way, to enable Fred to learn the road by driving. Fred was pleased about this. Then Bert showed the compassion he was known for, dropping down the tip-up seat and told his young fireman to sit down and watch.

With the signal 'Right away' from the Newport stationmaster, watched by four platform inspectors, three station foremen, numerous porters and the ladies who cleaned out the female powder rooms, Fred took *Farleigh Castle* out of the station and over the river bridge. As they passed Maindee East Junction, Bert put on the exhaust injector, pulled the pricker out of the rack and began to stir up the fire. They were passing Llanwern before he was satisfied that he had a good enough bed to build upon. They were now committed for better or for worse, non stop to Paddington, for with Royals on the back there would be no distant signal checks to help recovery should they run into trouble.

He began to fire her with all the experience that went back to the days of the 'Eight foot Singles'. First of all working on the back corners of the firebox, ramming it in with the shovel then building up under the firebox doors. He then put four good shovelfuls down to each front corner, six down the front end, six more straight down the middle, and now the hump of the 'haycock' fire began to take shape. This exercise continued, front, middle, back, until she stuck her nose down the incline into the Severn Tunnel.

Fred eased the regulator, tapping it down to the jockey valve. The water came down to half a glass, so Bert shut off the exhaust injector and gave her the live steam one to keep her from blowing off. They swooped down into the blackness, swallowing to ease the air pressure. The dank musty smell mingled with smoke, so familiar inside the Severn Tunnel, and drifted back into the cab. Bert was having a breather, there was no point in firing now, as she was far too rough to ride on, and she would only settle down when she was pulling.

The double white lights flashed by, and they were at the bottom of the tunnel. She then began to lift her nose, Bert stuck his thumb up, Fred nodded and opened her out and as the weight of the train caught her she settled down, beating strongly, the blast bouncing off the tunnel roof as she bit into the climb out. The firing began now with serious deliberation, up over the 'haycock' hump, front corners and down the middle. The brick arch was white hot with the gases whipping up over and through the tubes, the rich steam and smoke mixture filling the cab and being sucked back into the firebox. Each time the flap was dropped, the cab, the tender and first coach, were lit up sharply with a fierce golden flash, which reflected and was then thrown back from the dripping tunnel walls, and just as sharply shut off as the flap was raised.

They burst strongly out of the tunnel with the water level well up in the glass, and the steam pressure steady at 200 lb. Bert was able to shut down the blower, then open it up to a quarter of a turn, the chimney roaring away as they held the speed on the short section past Pilning. They then began the long climb up to Patchway, through the short tunnel, hammering away, with the blast threatening to tear the bricks out of the roof.

The dust began to fly as Bert came to some 'duff coal'. Within minutes they were all black and in his eagerness to please, the young fireman flew off the seat and began tearing into the coal with the coal pick, pulling it forward, breaking it, and passing it through his straddled legs so that Bert could shovel it in.

At Coalpit Heath the speed began to drop, then held at a steady lower pace as Fred dropped the lever down. At Chipping Sodbury they were dropping two minutes, but had enough speed to top up the water on the troughs. Then on through the long Sodbury tunnel until Badminton came into sight. Three minutes down now, but that awful drag up from the Severn was miles behind them.

As they came up to the station, Bert handed over the shovel to his laddie and told him to keep the fire just as it was. Two shovelfuls in each front corner, two more up the front, and six down the middle. He was to keep the back corners packed tight, making sixteen shovelfuls in all into that firebox. He could then hang out of the cab for a breather, long enough to count up to twelve, ready to start a round of the firebox again, feeding her as much as she would take. There was no danger of 'blacking in' that fire with fourteen thirty-five tonners on the back.

Fred gave up the regulator and stood behind Bert and watched. He had heard stories about Bert Edmonds and hard running, so there was now a chance to see this in practice. He knew that there were three minutes to make up, but, what he didn't know, and neither did George Price, was that Bert intended to make up another six minutes once he was back to normal running time. This was why he had built up such a fire and had emphasised to his fireman the importance of keeping it that way.

To Fred's surprise, Bert left the engine set as she was. She was running well and there was plenty of time to start her racing later on. Through Hullavington they had gained a minute, and although the climb up to Wootton Bassett and the restriction round the curve knocked some of the pace out of her, they made up another minute passing Rushey Platt. Bert eased down through Swindon but still retained the two minutes. Passing Highworth Box he opened her up again and began winding the lever back a notch at a time, feeling for her to respond, which she did. At Marston crossing that lost minute was found, and they were on time. George Price checked his watch and gave the 'thumbs up' to Bert. The young fireman began to enjoy himself, the fire was perfect, he had plenty of water in the boiler, and the pressure gauge was hovering at blowing off point. *Farleigh Castle* now began to fly as she had been designed to, racing across the Wiltshire Plain with the bit between her teeth.

They shot through Shrivenham like a flash, the cylinder pressure valve slapping like a machine gun with the first of Bert's six minutes in his pocket. His fireman packed in coal as he had been

y personal friend Bert
dmonds running the up
;ristolian' on a really
ismal day, seen here
pproaching the Milton
gnal box, near Didcot.
Author's collection

ert Edmonds and Vic
nith at Plymouth North
oad on 26th May 1956
ith 'Castle' class No.
)55 *Earl of Eldon* ready
leave with the up
imited'. This was Bert's
st trip before his retire-
ent.
Author's collection

A fine shot of Bert Edmonds at the regulator of 'Castle' class No. 5055 *Earl of Eldon.*

LAST TRAIN FROM PLYMOUTH
Driver A. J. Edmonds

After 44 years on the railways, an engine-driver made his last run from Plymouth to London today. He is Driver A. J. Edmonds, who comes from Tonbridge, Kent, and has been driving trains between Plymouth and London for the past five years.

An engine-driver on the Great Western and the Western Region of the British Railways for 32 years, now, atthe age of 65. Mr. Edmonds is retiring.

He told the "Herald" that throughout his 44 years on the railways he has never had a day's illness. He has driven all the crack trains on the Western Region, including the Cornish Riviera.

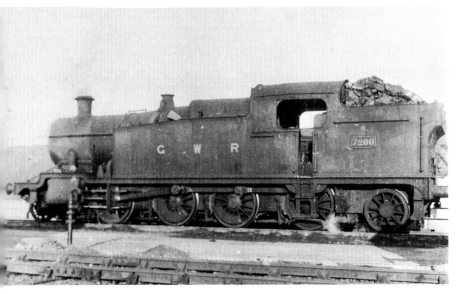

The very first 72XX tank. This one was to end up in Barry scrapyard.
Author's collection

'Castle' class No. 5012 *Berry Pomeroy Castle* waiting here at the Oxford up platform with only an hour's run to the capital.

OPC collection

'Castle' class No. 4025 showing signs of wear with steam coming from everywhere.

OPC collection

'Grange' class No. 6844 *Penhydd Grange* under pressure. Not one saved!

OPC collection

I even fired her. I remember the fine 'Lady'.

OPC collection

Home base! Now only the junction for Oxford and Swindon. Speeding through Didcot is 'Hall' class No. 4918 *Dartington Hall*.

OPC collection

What a superb nameplate! No. 5017 *The Gloucestershire Regiment 28th 61st* after renaming.

With only single pegging, 'King' class No. 6003 *King George IV* trundles slowly through Twyford.

OPC collection

The Royal Train crew leaving Chippenham with 'Castle' class No. 4091 *Dudley Castle* in charge of the 8.00 a.m. express from Weston-super-Mare.

Author's collection

'It's the one with the bell,' the lads all used to shout! 'King' class No. 6000 *King George V* seen here passing through Wellington with the 'Cambrian Coast Express'.

OPC collection

The 'King' again, here at Ruabon.

OPC collection

A 'King' at rest. Here at home in the works where she was made is 'King' class No. 6028 *King George VI*. What a monster!

OPC collection

Churchward's lovely big engine, the 47XX class, seen here with one of the class hauling an express on the relief line, near Twyford.

OPC collection

No. 5980 *Dingley Hall* flat out with the 14.20 Banbury freight.

OPC collection

The shed at rest.

OPC collection

No. 1455 at Swindon in 1964. I used to like these little engines, they worked well.
Dawlish Warren Railway Museum

No. 1442 about to leave Oxford with the local stopper to Princes Risborough.
OPC collection

Now *all* gone. Both the engine and station are no more.

OPC collection

No. 3769 stands at rest near the Swindon works turntable.

Dawlish Warren Rly Museum

No. 5511 leaves Swindon with a local stopper on a running in turn.

OPC collection

'Castle' class No. 7011 *Banbury Castle* getting up steam on Worcester shed.

OPC collection

Now in Swindon Railway Museum on view to all is *City of Truro*, seen here in service at Newbury in 1957.

OPC collection

A GWR tender, with driver and fireman taking a rest.

OPC collection

A good selection of signals seen from the footplate of a tender first tank.

OPC collection

The bit the shunter sees! No. 9000 backs on to its train at Machynlleth.

OPC collection

With a 'tankie' we never pass a water column!

OPC collection

GWR 'Castle' class No. 5081 *Lockheed Hudson* two and a half miles north of Oxford working the 9.17 Great Malvern to Paddington express, seen here on Sunday, 21st December 1958.

OPC collection

The steam man's delight! Diesels do burn as seen at the bottom of my garden near Oxford.

Author's collection

shown, and Fred in the well of the tender pulled the coal forward. As they roared through Uffington, Fred signalled to the lad to sit down, while he had a go at firing her. He was completely caught up in the excitement of what was going on. Another minute was gained through Challow and the third passing Steventon. George, up in the corner, was pleased. They were passing out of the Bristol Division into the London Division, and his report on the running of a 'Royal' would be a feather in the cap for Old Oak Common.

It was only when George realised that the usual four minutes between Steventon and Foxhall Junction had been cut to three that he began to know that something was up. They were running only just short of the 'Bristolian' timing, and shouted across the cab to Bert just as he pulled the whistle cord, as they approached Didcot. They hammered through the station, leaving porters clutching at their caps, drowning the station announcer on the tannoy, and setting the platform signs swinging and dancing as the displaced air rushed back in, with a cloud of dust.

Five minutes up as they passed Cholsey, George thought it about time to make a comment. He staggered across the bucking footplate and, placing his mouth against Bert's ear, he shouted, above the racket, that he knew that one member of the 'Royals' would enjoy 100 m.p.h. running with a steam engine, but that the 'Royal' that counted might not be so pleased. Bert grinned and eased the regulator down just to please him, for he knew that the odd minute he wanted would come. It did so as they swept through Goring and Streatley, as he could now afford to let her run as she was. He sat on the seat, swaying with the movement of the engine, and sucking away at his old pipe, knowing full well that George Price was muttering away up in the corner, wondering how they were going to lose six minutes with the road clear right into Paddington. When this run was over there would be some hard words on that footplate.

On up through the green sweep of Sonning Cutting they went and over Maidenhead bridge. Quickly sliding through Taplow and Burnham, they met the sweet sickly smells from the lineside factories of Slough, West Drayton, Hayes and Harlington. The fireman could sit down now, his work was over. A long pull was given on the whistle chain as they tore through the bridge and burst on the station at Southall. Bert was then rewarded with the sight he had been waiting for back at Newport, Hanwell distant signal at caution.

George stared with disbelief at that yellow light rushing towards them, as Bert shut off, and began giving *Farleigh Castle* short sharp bursts of the vacuum brake. The cab filled with the acrid aroma of hot brake blocks. As the blocks bit in, the speed dropped off sharply and as they came up to the viaducts, the reason for it all became clear. A big round sign at the lineside reading '15'.

They rumbled over, then Bert picked her up again making her bark her way through Hanwell, settling her down with a few winds on the lever. They marched on through Ealing Broadway and Acton, past Old Oak Common, then drifted under the bridge at Westbourne Park and rolled into Paddington, sedately coming to a stop with a final shot on the vacuum brake two yards away from those big shining stop blocks. The clock on the station wall gave a jerk with the hand bang on time.

For some moments that cab was completely quiet, broken only by the singing of the injector. George, Fred and the fireman were all stunned, but Bert sat there on his seat grinning like a Cheshire cat.

George came over and placed a hand on Bert's shoulder. Then he thanked him, admitting that he had completely forgotten all about that speed check at Hanwell, and without that high speed running, planned and worked for so many miles behind them, they would have been late with a 'Royal'.

A call from the platform from a well modulated voice made them turn round and look down, and there looking up into the cab was a tall gentleman dressed in the uniform of an Admiral of the Fleet. A bevy of less gold braid stood hovering with uncertainty behind him. He enquired as to which one of the four was the driver. Bert stood up and admitted that he was, and a clean white hand shot out from under a white cuff, and all that gold ringed uniformed sleeve, and firmly grasped Bert's grimy hand. He was congratulated for such a fine run and arriving 'on time'. It was then that Bert showed what compassion was all about, with a gesture typical of him. He brought his young fireman forward and said that this was the chap to be congratulated because, without his enthusiasm and hard work with the shovel, there would not have been enough steam to make such a fine run.

That laddie went home bursting with pride. His introduction to the 'Castle' class had not been a happy one to start with, coming as he did from the sedate pace and demands of a local working. That bucketing, swaying cab with its roaring fire and high speed running had been almost too much for him, but with Bert's tuition he had now had a taste of the 'runners' with one of the great men in Old Oak Common's Top Link, the gentle, understanding man, Bert Edmonds. The future held no terrors for that young fireman.

Royal Train working was of course nothing new to Bert. He shared this duty for many years with his old friend, driver Albert Potter. They shared the same starting date together, and would eventually share the same presentation dinner, given by their Old Oak Common colleagues in their honour, when it became time for them both to retire. But Royal Train working, or the experience necessary for this, started years before when they became firemen, in Bert's case, at Oxford.

A large number of the Old Oak Top Link men came from the country sheds, far removed from the sound of Bow Bells. They were more at home with the snort of a cow or the rough cough of a sheep, breaking the silence of the 2.00 a.m. walk to the shed. But surprising as it may seem, those country lads through a large number of different circumstances, found their true vocation in running the famous express trains on the premier routes of the Great Western.

Bert was no exception, as from the gentle branch trains to Fairford, Woodstock and Abingdon, he progressed on to the 'Singles', running to Worcester and Paddington. On these 'Singles' he worked with drivers such as Bill Soden, a big tough man who was as much at home in the ring, boxing the young University gentlemen, as he was on the footplate. Another was 'Cockney' Alf, his surname now forgotten, who differed from Bert, coming the other way to settle down in Oxford. When the 'Cities' took over from the 'Singles', Bert was firing to Frank Gleed, running trains at a speed he would become used to in later years.

A move now came, not to Old Oak, but to Cardiff Canton. Bert therefore moved his family and settled down in a little house on the outskirts of Cardiff at Ely. By good fortune his seniority brought him as a fireman on the 'runners', and it was during this period his vast knowledge of the road was built up. He already knew the road between Worcester, Hereford, Birmingham and Wolverhampton to Paddington, and as far west as Swindon. He was now firing to Swansea, Carmarthen and Fishguard to the west, Hereford and Shrewsbury to the north, and Bristol, Weston, and Taunton to the south. With the added bonus of the 'Castles' coming into service to complement the 'twenty-nines' and 'forties', it was a very exciting time, although at the time he would not have termed the run to Fishguard and back as such. He was sent to Swindon in 1930 for the driver's examination, and on passing, found that he was to fill a vacancy at Canton shed. He "crossed the footplate" and took over the regulator with some degree of thankfulness, but it was short lived. The excitement of the main line gave way to the Dock and Yard Pilots. The only relief from shunting up and down was a move up into the Valley link where Bert found that the "screw" or "pole lever" was there to go forward and back. The linking up of the valve gear was unheard of, simply because the gradients up into the Valleys did not allow it.

Railway footplate work in the Valleys was far removed from the main line, so far removed it was in a different world. Leaving Cardiff it was a case of blasting a way up to Tonypandy with the coal empties, shunting them to one side at the pit head, then starting the awful journey back down. This was a well planned operation from the start, and it had to be if the train was going to join the main line at Llantrisant, all in one piece. It was so easy to blow the code on the whistle for the signalman to set the points into the mile long sand trap, and hope to stop a run-away. The job of parting the train into many small portions to drag it out again for reforming was a long tedious operation, and the subject of an enquiry, so the planning to stop at Llantrisant began miles back at Tonypandy.

It started with the first move, moving the train out of the colliery yard at walking pace, never allowing the speed to build up. There would be two shunters, one on each side of the train, pinning down the wagon brakes using a brake stick to engage the handle, then with the weight of their body, they would bare down hard and engage the pin in the ratchet. This would go on all down the train, the engine working flat out against the weight of the train and the retarding effect of the brakes, until the driver was satisfied by the 'feel', that he had enough brakes down to hold them. A code sent on the whistle would then signal to the shunters, and from then on, they were on their own.

This was not a train movement for the timid driver, so Bert was glad of the foresight of the Cardiff shed foreman. For the first few days, he would allocate an experienced Valley fireman with a driver from the 'flat', just as the foreman at Old Oak would take care of an ex-Valley driver on the 'runners'. It was an arrangement not covered in any rule book, just a common sense understanding of railway working.

64

Bert took his time on that first trip, but even he was not pre-pared for the monumental weight that pushed him down the Valley. They rattled down through the little stations, blotting out everything behind the first wagon with a cloud of coal dust. Apart from the initial start, the regulator had been closed all the way, but he had made it safely thanks to his fireman's knowledge of working the handbrake. Bert had been lucky, it was a dry day, and Wales is renowned for rain. If the wheels had picked up on the locomotive there would have been a disaster. The Welsh engines were in tip-top condition with their sand boxes, and they worked. The ballast all the way down was covered with sand, so the occa-sions on which the trap was used, were few and far between.

In later years, when Bert passed a coal train plugging away up to Badminton on the main line, he would remember that to get there, someone had brought it down the valley, and he would mentally take his hat off in recognition of a duty as exacting as running a fast train.

Passenger working was again a different world. There were no short sharp bursts between stations with enough mileage to link up the valve gear and enjoy a little run, and no water troughs to top up the tank, so it was the practice never to pass a water column. There was one trip that was almost a merry-go-round, leaving Car-diff and up to Caerphilly, round the corner to Pontllanfraith, on to Crumlin High Level, across the high spindly bridge spanning the Western Valley Line, and into Pontypool, returning to New-port. With Valley stations in some instances within sight of one another, and restrictions as low as 5 m.p.h. due to colliery sub-sidences, the little gallop to Cardiff was welcomed. After hammer-ing the tank engines for an hour and a half, they had been working with the regulator open just long enough to shut it again. With margins so tight, Bert used to wonder how they ever kept time.

When the time came for Bert to move up into the next Link, it brought welcome relief, for it was back to the main line for most of the time. The jobs involved working freight trains to Neath and Swansea, 'vacuum' trains through to Fishguard, and local passengers into Bristol. The vast network of the Valleys was now under his hat along with all the main line knowledge, and yet he never gave it a thought. The shed foreman did when he checked the road book, as apart from the West of England, the routes that Bert had signed for, read like a dictionary.

Bert was one of those rare gentlemen who never knew when to say 'no'. To have a driver on the strength with that route availability was the answer to a foreman's prayer. This particularly was the case with the summer excursions, for the Welsh have a longing to visit London, and with most of Canton's Top Link men committed to the regular service, Bert was pressed into main line running at last.

It was a period that was to prove valuable in later years, but this main line running with excursions and extra parts of the booked trains, was done not with the benefit of the prime stud of Canton's locomotive power. For they, like their drivers, were already booked out as part of the Top Link working. Bert had to make do with the 'forties' and 'twenty-nines', but this was not as bad as it would at first seem. At this time in the early thirties, locomotives were kept in tip-top condition and burning the best steam coal available. After all, the Marine colliery was only a few miles away in the Western valley.

He took to the four cylindered 'forties' as a duck takes to water, preferring them to the 'Saints'. Although they were a very strong engine and would run, they were inclined to roll a bit at speed, but perhaps it was the speed he expected from them! When I was firing I never had the chance to find out, and to my regret I never had the chance to fire to Bert, but I heard all about him and his fast running.

In due course after a good spell at Canton, Bert set sail for Old Oak Common. Settling the family down in Saxton Road at Acton, Bert began to add route knowledge to the already phenomenal store he had in his head. He worked all round London's suburbia, running the local passengers and goods. He remembers with affection one of the little pannier tanks used on these jobs, because it had the names and nick-names of all the 262 drivers scratched in the paintwork of the cab. The names he can remember are well worth mentioning because of the humour of the unknown sign-writer. Charlie Shave was 'Barber', Bob Goddard was 'The Vicar', Bert himself was 'Smiler', but the classic must go to Charlie Noller, known as 'Rice pudding Charlie'.

Humour was part and parcel of sheds and enginemen. There was a period when the foreman decided to have a purge on departure times from Old Oak, insisting that all engines leaving the shed must be timed and the name of the driver given to the signalman. It was a failure from the start, as every engine leaving after 6.00 a.m. was driven by driver Charlie Hutchings, so that when 8.00 a.m. came round and fifty-odd engines had left the shed the inevitable happened — as all the previous drivers knew it would — the real

Charlie Hutchings came along. It was only after a telephone call to the shed and an irate foreman had come to identify Charlie, that the exasperated signalman allowed him to leave the shed, with the promise from the foreman that name taking had come to an end.

Bert moved on up through the links, running goods and passengers. With the war now upon us he had the worries shared by most drivers. Long hours spent on trains, his children away in the Services, and his dear wife Annie alone in the house during all the bombing. But, thank goodness, they all came through unscathed although there were some close shaves, and when it was over, Bert found himself working the vacuum fitted trains down to the West Country. The working again kept him away from home because all these jobs involved an overnight stay, 'double home' as it was termed, but he enjoyed the runs. The 11.40 p.m. from Paddington Goods was a particular favourite. They left Paddington, called in at Old Oak yard, then ran non-stop to Tiverton Junction, where they put off a dozen box vans for the Duchess of Cornwall Creamery. The next stop was Newton Abbot where they booked off.

The locomotives used on these workings were always one of the big 'forty-seven' class, and Bert enjoyed running them as they should be run. He said that they 'wouldn't half roll' down the other side of Savernake, and they would scoff the coal, but his firemen didn't mind. Bert never thrashed an engine unless it was necessary, and he always took a turn on the shovel.

Bert came into the Top Link just about the time that the wartime speed restrictions were being lifted, and at last he got his hands on the 'Kings'. It was with this locomotive that some passengers who made regular runs behind them, began to take notice and start timing, for the combination of Bert Edmonds and a 'King' was a formidable one. When I pressed him as to which 'King' was his favourite he was quick to remember. No. 6014 *King Henry VII* was a marvellous engine, No. 6026 *King John* was in a class of its own, but pride of place went to No. 6000 *King George V*. Bert made no bones about it, his footplate at Paddington was a 'Mecca' for small boys when he had the 'George'. He was fortunate in having the finest firemen at Old Oak, for as he said, he couldn't have made those fine runs without them. They were so good that 20 years afterwards he could recall some of their names with affection. There was Dick Bedford, Vic Smith, Tom Ward, Tom Pitt, Danny Tobin, and, when he could pinch him off his old mate driver Albert Potter, he would enjoy the company of Jack Peedell.

It was while he was with Danny Tobin that Bert started a leg-pull that went a bit further than he had intended. It did no harm but it caused some serious heart searching by quite a few senior drivers, not only at Old Oak Common, but all over the Great Western Railway.

For a long time a rumour had been floating about the sheds that drivers would have to pass an examination on the operating rules again. This was an examination taken only by the firemen going to Swindon to pass out as drivers, which meant that they could be called upon to carry out driving duties while still being employed as firemen. They would undergo a further examination to pass out as fully qualified drivers, and that would be the end of it throughout their careers. The very idea that senior drivers would have to pass again after so many years was unthinkable. The only time that they went to Swindon was to pass a medical on reaching the age of sixty, and on each subsequent year until they retired at sixty-five.

This medical examination was brought in during 1951, and it so happened that Bert became the first man to go. He went to work that day in his best suit, booking on in the shed just the same as if it were a duty. It was in fact classed as such. He collected his pass and caught the empty coaches up to Paddington. There he had a cup of tea in the canteen where he received a lot of leg pulling from the youngsters about the 'old folk' and good wishes from them all. But each man was with him, for it was not unknown for senior drivers to come off the footplate through ill health. Bert had no worries over that score, as far as he knew, but doctors are likened to vets, they are a queer lot, and he did have that row of bullet holes up his leg, a legacy from World War One.

Bert caught the train and settled down for the ride to Swindon. Now and again he pulled out his watch to check the running times until he remembered that this was a bad habit, only practised by the retired section sitting on park benches, all the way from London to Plymouth. When he arrived at Swindon he walked down the road to the Park Road headquarters, musing over the thought that the twenty odd years since he had last come this way, seemed only a few years ago.

Bert sailed through that medical as he was to do each year until he retired. He caught the train home in high spirits, and it was while he was in this mood the seeds were sown. 'Old folk' indeed — he would give them something to think about, and that was an understatement.

68

Walking down to the shed, he met a driver who quite naturally asked him how he had got on at Swindon. Bert replied that he had passed the medical without any trouble, but that the operating rules had made him scratch his head. Having dropped this bit of information into the hands of a bloke he knew would make the most of it, he quietly booked off and slid home.

Bert's next duty was on a Sunday morning two days after the Swindon visit. He walked into Old Oak shed with Danny Tobin all ready to prepare No. 5066 *Sir Felix Pole* for an excursion to Gloucester. Old Oak shed even on a Sunday was a busy place, but the first thing they noticed was the lack of activity and one driver was obviously waiting for them. He was Bert Collins, the chap who ran the Mutual Improvement Classes on operating rules and locomotive failures, (for the benefit of firemen aspiring to pass the examinations for promotion to driver) and he knew Bert for the leg-puller that he was.

He asked the same question that the other driver had asked two days previously, how Bert got on at Swindon? Bert replied, leaving out the bit about being the first to be taken on the rules. Bert Collins was not satisfied and pressed a bit harder and wheedled out of Bert that perhaps he had mentioned to someone a little snippet about rule examinations. That explained the quiet shed, for Bert Collins had completely sold out of every kind of rule book and engine book that he had in stock. He said that if driver Bert Edmonds was to look inside the engineman's cabin, he would find at least thirty drivers and senior firemen, all sitting in a row with their heads in their hands, poring over the rule books laid on the table in front of them.

Bert decided to move with discretion. He got Danny to go to the locker and obtain his preparation overalls, but told him not to breathe a word that he was in the shed. He changed on the footplate while Danny went to the stores for the oil, then Bert slipped underneath *Sir Felix Pole* and oiled the inside motion. Danny worked hard to raise enough steam to move her, then they crept outside and found a quieter spot where Bert could finish his oiling. For once Bert did not go to the cabin for a wash, he cleaned up in a bucket on the footplate, then as soon as they were ready they slipped out of Old Oak shed and up to Paddington.

Bert breathed a big sigh of relief. It would be getting dark when they returned so he could dodge the odd driver, and the next day he was on the 'Limited' so he would leave from Paddington and not be back until late Tuesday afternoon. By then it would have all blown over. They ran *Sir Felix Pole* and her train full of W.I. ladies to Gloucester enjoying the super run with a light load. On arrival they shunted the coaches into the sidings and dropped onto the shed, their work completed until the return run in the afternoon.

Danny had run the fire down so he dropped the dampers, filled up the boiler so that she would stand for a few hours without any attention, then they went to the cabin for a wash and a cup of tea. Here they expected a quiet chat with the Gloucester lads, but those lads had no time for a chat, they were all busy studying the rule book. Bert beat a hasty retreat to *Sir Felix Pole* whilst Danny made the tea, and there he stopped for his break. He then spent the rest of the afternoon sitting on a park bench well away from drivers who might ask awkward questions.

The oiling of *Sir Felix Pole* ready for the return was made with the same stealth as at Old Oak. Danny curled up with laughter at Bert creeping round with an oil feeder in his hand, lowering his head at the sight of any person dressed in overalls. He had no sympathy for Bert. One of his leg-pulls had backfired. Once on the road and heading for home, Bert brightened up and began to sing, as the immediate danger was over. Danny was driving and Bert was enjoying himself on the shovel. He had it all worked out, as they were dropping on to the ash road at Old Oak, Danny could put *Sir Felix Pole* to bed, and he would creep off and catch the Underground to Acton. And that's how he got away with it.

Monday came round and they both set off for the West with the 'Limited', hauled by No. 6026 *King John* with the usual full load. They made a fine sight in the sunshine as they swept round the curve at Reading Main Line West Junction, canting over against the curve, but running smoothly so as not to tip the soup into the laps of the diners in the restaurant car. Bert had a good reputation with the waiters, they could serve soup without any trouble when he was driving. He waved to his brother-in-law Bill Gasson who was down in the yard of Reading shed, waiting for him to go by. He expected a cheery wave in reply but instead caught sight of a clenched fist waving at him. Bert felt a little sad. What had he done to upset old Bill? Danny was leaning over his shoulder, one hand on the water scoop handle, grinning like a cat. He knew Reading had heard about rule examinations. Bert sniffed and stuffed his old pipe full, the further he left Old Oak behind the further he left the trouble.

Easing down at Newbury for a speed restriction, he rolled

through at 20 m.p.h. looking out for me and my old dad on the Winchester passenger standing in the bay. We were waiting for him, and both of us held a rule book high in our hands, and the naughty code known to all enginemen was blown on the whistle. Bert replied with the two finger salute while Danny had both his hands round Bert's throat as if to strangle him. Danny still had that wide grin on his face, it was a situation he was enjoying immensely. The number one Top Link Driver at Old Oak was a fugitive, but Bert was not one to give up. The whistle code was returned, then he opened up *King John* marching her up towards Enborne Junction with the bit between her teeth. Surely, he thought, he would be safe from the Great Western jungle drums in Plymouth.

They ran into Plymouth North Road on time as usual with Bert. In his eyes a speed restriction way back at Newbury was no excuse to run in late. When they arrived in the shed they again noticed the lack of drivers and firemen. In the cabin they found the now familiar sight of enginemen deep in study, rule books in front of each one.

Danny decided to risk a question. Why were rule books now the centre of such interest? The reply he received rocked poor old Bert back on his heels. Surely they'd heard, some unfortunate driver had been the first to go to Swindon under the new arrangements. He had passed the medical all right but he had failed on the rules, so they had taken him off the footplate and put a broom in his hand and now the poor old chap was pushing that broom up and down in the pits.

All of this came out with such conviction it must have been true and the local Union representative was going to bring it up at the meeting on Sunday morning. Bert made the usual noises in agreement, in fact he almost believed it himself. When he looked round for Danny's support he found him missing. Danny was outside, had he remained, he would have given the game away by laughing. Bert began to worry a bit now, a simple remark to one man back at Old Oak had swept right through the Great Western locomotive world, and he could not stop it, but neither could he admit to starting it.

Danny had the answer, for once he was in a position to be able to advise Bert how to go on. His advice was, to keep quiet and act naturally, and hope and pray that Bert Collins would keep his mouth shut. Bill Gasson at Reading would keep his mouth shut, and Harold Gasson senior and Harold Gasson junior at Didcot would also, but Danny, Bert could rely on, as he was his mate.

But as Danny explained, it was a big burden to carry, and he would consider it over a few jars always providing that Bert paid.

As rumours begin so they end, and this one was no exception. Within a few weeks another driver was sent to Swindon and he found that the medical was the only examination he had to pass. Bert was once again able to walk into the shed with his head held high as befits a Top Link driver. This yarn has remained a secret until now, 28 years later.

As each year went by, Bert continued to pass his medical. He loved every minute on the 'runners', sweeping along the sea wall at Dawlish, waving to the kids on the path and pressing himself up in the cab during the winter when the sea came crashing over the engine. There was the hard run to Wolverhampton with its tight timings which was part and parcel of the route, and hammering up through Saunderton Tunnel or sweeping down through Bicester with the pressure valves spanking away, and miles and miles of straight fast running down to Gerrards Cross. He loved that bit of railway because 'they wouldn't half "tank" along' by which he meant, that they were going as fast as he dare let them.

But one day it had to come to an end, and with it a record that would be hard to beat. Bert had completed 44 years on the footplate without once being away sick or late on duty. His last day at work was 26th May 1956.

His last trip was with the Down 'Limited', returning the next day with the 10.0 a.m. from Penzance. Such was his standing at Old Oak that when he arrived to book on for the last time, the foreman offered him a choice of four 'Castles' from which to choose. They were lined up ready, the night shift cleaners had polished them all up, and the young day shift lads were waiting for him to choose before they gave that locomotive the final shine. He could choose from No. 5040 *Stokesay Castle*, No. 5066 *Sir Felix Pole*, No. 5069 *Isambard Kingdom Brunel*, and No. 5055 *Earl of Eldon*.

Bert walked round them carefully, taking his time so as not to disappoint either the foreman, or any of the lads who had been so considerate. His fireman, Vic Smith, followed him. He had his own ideas as to which was the best 'Castle' as it was a long way to Plymouth and back. Bert told me that the choice was a very difficult decision to make. He had worked *Stokesay Castle* the week before and she was a good engine but she was becoming a rough rider. *Sir Felix Pole* was not so free steaming although she rode like a coach. *Isambard Kingdom Brunel* was the strongest 'Castle' he had handled and she was like an old friend, but *Earl of Eldon* was just about the best 'Castle' in the whole fleet at Old Oak. So Bert chose her much to the relief of Vic, who also preferred her.

Good news travels fast in railway circles, as well as bad news, but Bert was quite unprepared for the reception that was waiting for him at Paddington. The Station Master was there as indeed he would be on the return trip, and lined up on the platform waiting to shake his hand was the complete restaurant car staff. Those Old Oak drivers using the canteen were on the footplate, and a hoard of small boys were waiting to obtain the signature of one of the Royal Train drivers while there was still time. At last the shrill sound of whistles sounded down the platform and Bert opened the large ejector to boost the small one. There was a scramble to leave the footplate, and as the last lad climbed down, Bert gave a blast on the whistle, opened up the regulator, and for the very last time took the 'Limited' out of Paddington.

Earl of Eldon barked her way past Westbourne Park. From Paddington Departure box to Old Oak Common East and West boxes, the signalmen were waving from the windows. In Old Oak yard the shunting engines were pulling down both brake and train whistles. The foreman and Shed foreman had brought every member of the shed staff with them. Drivers, firemen, cleaners, boilersmiths, fitters, mates, firedroppers, and the lads from the coal stage, all lined up to see Bert take the 'Limited' out.

I think it was at that time that Bert realised that he was someone special. He had never before thought about it, but now he began to wish there were a few more years left. He linked the 'Earl' up, stuffed his old pipe full and settled down, slipping through Southall almost before he noticed. Then he remembered, the big diesels were coming in, and although Bert knew they would be clean to work on, he wanted nothing to do with them. The next generation, like his fireman Vic, could take care of them.

Bert eased down for the run round the curve at Reading. From old habit he looked down into the yard of Reading shed to see if Bill Gasson was about. He was there all right, and so was every member of the Reading staff that Bill could collect together. To a person outside railway circles it must have seemed as if the Royal Train was going through.

The jungle drums were still working as he ran through Newbury and at every signal box window the lads were waving. Bert began to wish he was making his last run on the 'Bristolian' as he had to look out at every box in case he missed someone, so he talked Vic into taking over the driving while he had his fling on the shovel.

Earl of Eldon ran like a sewing machine. She must have known it was Bert's last Down trip. They ran into Plymouth dead on time, as it had been one of those perfect runs so well remembered. The foreman was there to greet Bert and said that he had another 'Castle' for him to take back the next morning if Bert would like to. So he went with Vic to have a look at her. She was No. 5025 *Chirk Castle* and she was immaculate as only a 'Castle' can look when groomed to perfection.

Bert was deeply moved with this offer but he said as gently as he could that he would like to take *Earl of Eldon* home with him. She was taken over to the ash road where her fire was cleaned and her tender filled. While Bert and Vic were away for the night they coaled her with first grade coal, the tender was trimmed, the coal all broken up into nice size lumps for Vic to use, and the night turn cleaners shone her up, just as their opposite numbers at Old Oak had done the night before. When Bert and Vic came on duty that next morning she was all ready to take off the shed, and would have done credit to a 'Royal' train.

Their departure was a repetition of the day before. Every man and boy on the shed lined up to shake Bert's hand and wish him well, and when he backed on to his coaches in the station, the Press were there to record the moment. Had Bert known what was in store for him at Paddington, he would have swopped for a night duty to end his driving days. The Press at Plymouth was just a fore-taste of what was waiting for him. Vic had an idea as he had been primed, but he was too good a mate to tell him, his dear old mate Bert was entitled to a good send off.

Bert took the 'Earl' out of Plymouth sighing with relief. It had been nice to receive the good wishes from his old mates, but he was a quiet, shy man, not used to having photos taken by the Press, and having so many questions fired at him. He was pleased though that he had been promised copies of the papers, his dear Annie would be so thrilled.

The run home over the switchback road of the West Country was just as sweet as the run down had been. As the familiar country-side wound past Bert got to musing. They reached a section where they had run a tender box hot, and there was the spot where the wind had whipped his cap off. There was the place where *King George V* had nearly jumped the rails when a rail had broken. Bert began to feel a bit morbid, as it was the last trip, and never again would he feel the warmth of the regulator in his hand, and the strong heart beats of a 'Castle' or a 'King' pounding out through those four cylinders. He tapped Vic on the shoulder and beckoned him over to the right hand side, it was time he had his last fling on the shovel.

For an hour, Bert fired *Earl of Eldon* enjoying himself as a sixty five year old should never have been capable of doing. Bert might have reached retiring age in the eyes of the Railway, but in fact, he was fitter than a lot of forty year olds. Regular firing and using a spade in an enormous allotment had kept him that way.

That last run seemed almost too quick to be true as they swept off the curve at Reading West Main and up through the middle road. Twyford, Maidenhead, Taplow, Burnham and Slough slipped by. West Drayton, Southall and Ealing Broadway came rushing up towards them at such a speed, that Bert knew the moment was almost upon him, when he would have to shut that regulator. He took her through Acton still taking steam, then between Old Oak box and Westbourne Park the moment had to come or he would go right through Paddington and end up in Praed Street. Down it went, up with the clip, and the reverser was wound down. Bert was far too busy now to think of anything else, he had to reduce her speed. He made short sharp bursts on the vacuum brake, letting the pump restore the reservoir then more brake soon brought the speed down, filling the cab once more with the acrid smell of the hot brake blocks.

They ran past Ranelagh Bridge with its line of engines waiting to creep up to Paddington. Under the bridge, and rounding the curve and the criss-cross of cross-overs with the wheels' flanges squealing in protest, they were soon gliding into the great cavern of Paddington with its honking taxi horns and the voice booming on the tannoy.

The vacuum brake went on, killing the last few turns of the wheels. Bert checked his pocket watch against the station clock and noticed, with satisfaction, that he had arrived half a minute before time. He looked back at the passengers spilling out, then turned towards the 'Lawn' to see a sight he had seen so many times before. British Movietone News people were gathered there with cameras and sound recording equipment together with BBC television. The sound engineers were running to keep up with the interviewer and cameramen, while a whole gaggle of newspapermen struggled to get past them.

Bert remarked to Vic that there must be a famous film star on board. This was a common sight at Paddington and Bert had seen them all, but as he turned towards Vic it was to see him sliding out of the cab and round the corner to stand on the framing. He was replaced by his old mate Albert Potter wearing a wide grin on his face, closely followed by the station master complete with his top hat. Following them came the Old Oak foremen and two loco running inspectors, Frank Wheeler and Charlie Darrel-Smith.

Albert Potter had run in on his last trip with the Up 'Swansea' some time before, and as he shook Bert's hand, it suddenly dawned on Bert that all this fuss was not for some glamorous young starlet, but for Albert Potter and himself. It was a reporter's delight, the two Great Western Royal Train drivers retiring, and both on the footplate together.

The situation on the footplate of *Earl of Eldon* had become impossible. Bert could not remember how it happened, but somehow he found himself on the platform with Vic on one side, and Albert Potter and his fireman Jack Peedel on the other. He was thrown to the wolves, as he later said, but the reporters were far from being the tough, hard men they were cracked up to be. They could see that both Albert and Bert were quiet, shy men, far more at home hustling the 'Bristolian' along at one hundred miles an hour, than facing them. So they treated them with consideration, and although both men were bemused with the flash bulbs going off and the microphones wagging back and forth between them, the skill of the reporting brought out everything that was required.

They found themselves in the coaches of the 'Limited' that Bert had brought up from the West Country, riding back to Old Oak. Bert hadn't been relieved and he worried about it, until Charlie Darrel-Smith assured him that he had arranged for a crew to take over. They had climbed quietly up on to the 'Earl' from the fireman's side while Bert and Vic were on the platform, so Bert settled down for the short ride back to Old Oak Common Shed.

It was some time before he could get away, there were so many 'goodbyes' to be said, and in any case, he would be back in the shed within a few days to clear out his locker. At last he was allowed to go, but there was just one more thing to do. He walked back up towards the ash road with his arm around Vic's shoulders, back to where he would find *Earl of Eldon*.

She stood there, quiet now, simmering gently, her boiler pressure down to a hundred pounds, at rest. In the setting sun the gloss of her deep Brunswick green paintwork showed the thin film of dust and flattened flies from her four hour run. A gentle trickle of water dribbled out of the injector waste pipe, splashing quietly on to the charred sleepers. Bert climbed up on to the footplate, crossed over to his seat of two hours ago, and sat down.

He was not normally a sentimental man where steam locomotives were concerned, but he had a fine feeling for a beautiful machine. He could sense its moods and match those feelings so as to obtain the very best in performance. It was a feeling shared by most of the Top Link drivers all over the Western, but there was no time for sentiment in the normal turmoil of running an express train. This visit back to the footplate was quite out of character for Bert, it was just something he had to do. He lit up his pipe and sat there quietly in the twilight for half an hour, puffing away as he listened to the gentle sounds of the 'Earl' settling down, thinking back over the years to when he began on an eight foot 'Single' at Oxford.

Vic sat on the other seat without speaking, for he felt that to disturb Bert now would have been sacrilege. He knew, too, that on the footplate of No. 5004 *Llanstephan Castle* standing behind them, Albert Potter sat there in the gloom. Two silent men buried deep in the memories of the past, each in his way making his peace with that part of his life that was over.

At last Bert got up, slid open the firebox doors and knocked out his pipe. He touched Vic on the shoulder, then he was gone.

I have never shown Bert any photographs of the massacre at Barry scrap yard. He knew it happened and it saddened him, but he felt much better when I told him that *Earl of Eldon* was not rusting away in a seaside scrap yard, covered in bird droppings and the playthings of countless children from the nearby holiday camp. She had gone home to Swindon where she was built, and had been dismantled with care on the 19th October 1964.

It pleased him to think that No. 6000 *King George V* had been saved, and that I had fired her, and that so many others had been saved from the cutter's torch. When I told him that No. 5051 *Earl Bathurst* was at Didcot and well on the way to main line running again, his reaction was one of unbounding enthusiasm. I can only hope that one day I can bring him to Didcot and once again place him on the footplate of a 'Castle'.

I saw you lying in the scrapyard, doomed to slow decay,
Stripped of your brass and copper, weeds around your rusting
  frame,
And I was moved to tears, as I recalled the day,
When you were beautiful, and bore a shining name.

To me you were perfection with your clean uncluttered line,
Gave you a touch of class that only Swindon could design,
I see again your copper banded chimney, your livery of green,
Your gleaming cab-side number plate, your bright red buffer
  beam.

Mine was the hand that gave you power and speed,
Turned fire and water into breath that you might live,
I toiled to minister your every need,
I gave you all the loyalty I had to give.

Seduced by smell of steam, hot oil, wrapped in your warm
  embrace,
Enchanted thus, I fed the fire that burned in you,
With your pulsating beat, my happy heart kept pace,
As down the track with flashing rod on speeding wheels we flew.

And as we sped along, you whispered to me,
Of joys to come, when I your master, not your slave, would be,
Sometimes you mocked me, your shrill laughter borne upon the
  wind,
But I was young, and dedicated, so I did not mind.

Sadly, you could not fulfil the promise that you gave,
For time and progress bore you to this open grave,
I cannot rouse you now, cold forlorn you lie,
Such poetry in motion once, Why did you have to die?

Wild was your song of steam that I accompanied,
Its roaring rhythm in my ears,
Though now your fire is gone, your pulse, your voice is still,
I hear the music that we made, come echoing down through the
  years.

Clare Sellen
1.3.78